TRUE WHIT

TRUE WHIT

DESIGNING A LIFE OF STYLE, BEAUTY, AND FUN

Whitney Port

with *Sheryl Berk*

itbooks

AN IMPRINT OF HARPERCOLLINS PUBLISHERS

Grateful acknowledgment is made to the following for the use of photographs: pp. ii, x, 6, 22, 38, 43, 46, 79, 101, 122, 123, 144, 156, 157, 162, 174, 176, and 224: © Simon Biswas; pp. vi and 84: courtesy of Rebecca Taylor; Whitney Port and Lauren Conrad, p. 41: © Jason Merritt/Getty; Whitney Port, Roxy Olin, and Kelly Cutrone, p. 41: © Steve Granitz/Getty; p. 51: © Larry Busacca/Getty; p. 63: © Justin Campbell/Getty; p. 66: © Alli Harvey/Getty; black boots, p. 84: courtesy of Dr. Martens; jeans, pp. 84 and 108: courtesy of Genetic Denim; p. 90: © Jesse Grant/Getty; p. 91: © Isaac Brekken/Getty; Whitney Port in evening gown, p. 92: © Kevin Mazur/Getty; Whitney Port in cocktail dress, p. 92: © Michael Tran/Getty; p. 93: © Gustavo Caballero/Getty; Whitney Port in cut-out dress, p. 94: © Rebecca Sapp/Getty; Whitney Port in printed dress, p. 94: © George Pimentel/Getty; Whitney Port in jeans, p. 95: © Jeffrey Mayer/Getty; Whitney Port in red dress, p. 95: © Mark Sullivan/Getty; p. 96: courtesy of Hanky Panky; p. 97: courtesy of Belabumbum; p. 107: © George Pimentel/Getty; p. 110: © Theo Wargo/Getty; p. 150: courtesy of Baked by Melissa; p. 167: courtesy of Enjoy Professional Haircare; pp. 182 and 183: courtesy of Fresh; p. 183: courtesy of bareMinerals; p. 186: © Mark Sullivan/Getty; p. 206: © Randy Brooke/Getty; p. 223: © Gustavo Caballero/Getty. All other photos courtesy of the author or publisher.

HarperCollins books may be purchased for educational, business, or sales promotional use. For information please write: Special Markets Department, HarperCollins Publishers, 10 East 53rd Street, New York, NY 10022.

FIRST EDITION

Designed by Ashley Halsey

Library of Congress Cataloging-in-Publication Data
Port, Whitney, 1985–
True Whit : designing a life of style, beauty, and fun / Whitney Port, with Sheryl Berk. — 1st ed.
    p.   cm.
  ISBN 978-0-06-199686-3
    1. Young women—Life skills guides. 2. Fashion. 3. Beauty, Personal. 4. Dating (Social customs). 5. Career development. I. Berk, Sheryl. II. Title.
  HQ1229.P76 2011
  646.70084'22—dc22
                                                2010016983

11 12 13 14 15   OV/QG   10 9 8 7 6 5 4 3 2 1

To the family whose love has given me the will and the courage to fly.
To Mommy, Daddy, Bucka, Boppa, Ry, Ash, Paige, and Jade:
Your love has brought harmony to my life.
Without you this dream would not be alive.

CONTENTS

TRUE WHIT

INTRODUCTION

My mom always called it the "quarter-life crisis," the time in your life when you're in your twenties, out of school, and facing the world on your own for the first time. To be honest, it didn't sound like a crisis to me; it sounded pretty great. Freedom, an amazing career, finding the man of my dreams . . . I couldn't wait to be on my own. I could do what I wanted, be what I wanted, dress like I wanted, and spend my money on *anything*. Crisis? It sounded like heaven!

So in August 2008, a year after finishing college at the University of Southern California, I packed up my clothes, shoes, and accessories (enough to probably fill two apartments!) and moved to New York City to start my life and make it as a fashion designer. I found my first place in the Flatiron District, and the freedom felt incredible. Okay, it wasn't exactly the sophisticated New York apartment I'd envisioned. In fact, it was on the thirtieth floor (I am semiscared of heights), the ceilings were superlow, and my closet was the size of a shoebox. But it was still mine, all mine, and my first night in it, I felt invincible. I furnished it by scouring the floors of ABC Carpet, hitting up the local flea market and thrift shops, shopping online for basic must-haves, as well as finding some of the accessories at antique stores in Osage Beach, Missouri (a spot my family has traveled to since the year I was born).

I distinctly remember lighting a candle, ordering Chinese food, and using boxes as tables to have a romantic night with my boyfriend when I first moved in.

I was lucky in these tough financial times to also land a job right away as a public relations assistant for the Diane von Furstenberg brand. DVF is such an incredible designer, I simply wanted to work there and was willing to do anything and everything just to be a part of the team. However, my job was not exactly the glamorous fashion position I'd imagined. It consisted of a lot of assistant tasks—like searching the media for celebs wearing DVF, dressing the mannequins, assisting in seating charts for runway shows—and required little creativity. I felt like I was going nowhere fast. At twenty-three years old, I shouldn't have expected much more responsibility; I just knew I was capable of so much more. Don't get me wrong: I owe DVF immensely for her words of empowerment and the time she spent making sure I followed my dreams. But . . .

After a few weeks of experiencing my newfound freedom, I began to think maybe Mama was on to something. Being on my own wasn't as easy as I thought. The real world is filled with challenges, expectations, pressure, and to be honest, more than a few crazy people. I wish they taught a class on this in college: Real Life 101. Maybe then I would have known what to expect and how to handle it with grace and style and less stress. Instead, I had to find my way. I had to experience firsthand what it's like to be in a relationship with Mr. Not Quite Right and to work with someone vying for the title "Wicked Witch of the East." I had to stuff envelopes and answer phones and fetch coffee and steam fabric and lug bins of clothes. And even harder: I had to figure out how to look *good* even when things were really bad.

There were times I would have loved to just throw in the towel, to crawl back home to my parents and be a kid again with no responsibilities, no rent to pay, no repercussions for showing up five minutes late to a work meeting without a pen. I wish someone would have warned me that bills pile up, jobs are never as good as they sound on Monster.com, and not everyone at the office is nice (some are shockingly biased and backstabbing!). Sometimes I didn't know who to trust or where to turn. I missed the comforts of college and home; I felt anxious, overwhelmed, *alone*. One day, I woke up in a cold sweat wondering, *where am I going? And will I ever get there?* I was in . . . a crisis.

But here's the kicker: I got to experience my quarterlife crisis in front of *millions* of people every week! MTV's *The City* is a great show, and I'm really proud of it, but it's also *really* revealing. Sometimes, I feel like I'm living in a fishbowl and there are

But it's not *only* me. I know that it's my real-life problems that so many girls relate to—they tell me so all the time. They say they're rooting for me, and because of that, I can't give up. So that's what I did: I took a deep breath and reassessed. I made good friends and weeded out the frenemies. I tried three new jobs until I found one that felt right. I decided to pursue my original dream of being in fashion, even if it meant taking a huge leap of faith and risking failure. I surrounded myself with a support team who believed

Think of this book as your road map to discovering what you want in life and how to make it happen.

things, frankly, I wish the whole wide world didn't have to see. Most of the week, I have cameras in my face filming everything— and I mean *everything*. The good, the bad, and the "Oh, my God! I can't believe I did that!" So there I was, new to New York, being on my own and working while the cameras captured me failing, falling on my butt, and freaking out. The producers were probably thrilled—I became a drama magnet and I always said I never would be one. I even lived out a serious relationship and painful breakup over several episodes. As my friend Roxy Olin would say, "Only you, Whit, only you . . ."

in me, and even better, I discovered how important it was to believe in myself. If you stay true to who you are, you'll eventually (I promise!) stumble across the right path.

So that's the road I am hopefully on now. If you've watched me on *The Hills* or *The City*, you know it hasn't been easy getting here, and I absolutely expect more bumps along the way. But what you've seen on the shows is only the half of it; many of my experiences wind up on the cutting-room floor (we only have thirty minutes per episode, after all). So this book is the *true* Whit: all the situations I've been through and survived, all the solutions that worked for me as well as the ones that didn't. I felt there was so much more that I could share beyond what you

hair (I can put my face on in five minutes flat, I swear!). Then there's the *really* useful stuff you need to know, like how to recover

Starting out is like being on a roller coaster. You know there are going to be some terrifying twists and turns, and you might feel scared or even sick to your stomach at times, but the thrill of the ride takes your breath away.

see on the show. What I wanted to create was a guidebook, so to speak, to starting out in your twenties. This is a hard time in your life to navigate—sometimes it can feel impossible to have fun and not stress out while you're trying to get the hang of being "a grown-up." It was particularly hard for me, because I live most of my life in the public view. If I stayed out all night with friends partying, not only would I have my boss and coworkers to contend with in the morning, I also knew the cameras would be rolling. This forced me to learn some tricks for quick makeup and

from a hangover, find the perfect outfit when you're having dinner with an ex, and throw a fabulous last-minute dinner party using just a toaster oven!

If you're anything like me, you've probably got a million questions: "What's my passion? "Where do I want to be in five years?" "*Now* what?" I can't answer these questions for you, but I can give you some great tools to start figuring them out. I've also been lucky enough throughout my journey so far to have met really dynamic people who are really good at what they do: stylists, trainers, business execs—and also my friends and family. They're all in here, sharing their words of wisdom. They are the roots that have allowed me to grow.

People are always asking me for advice (I guess that's what I get for being on a reality TV show!): "Whitney, what should I do now that I've graduated from college?" Well, here (after much personal trial and error!) is what I have to say to that:

- Dream big, dearies, and dress the part!
- Live the life you love and don't be afraid to take chances!
- Be fabulous, be fearless, be yourself!

And yes, you're going to screw up. I sure did, and I will continue to do so. But that's okay. Mistakes are good things, even if they don't feel like it at the time (try to remember that when you're sobbing on the phone to your bestie). They make you wiser and stronger. They help put things into perspective, like what really counts (the people you love who love you back) and what really doesn't (your burned dinner, your fashion faux pas, your flaky blind date). They teach you how to cope and not crumble.

You also need to give yourself a break. *Seriously!* There seems to be this big misconception that because you're in your twenties and a "grown-up" now, you're supposed to have your entire life figured out. That's *so* not true; I know very few twentysomethings who have all their stuff together. Up until now—for the past twenty-plus years—your entire life has been on a strict schedule. So this is the first time you're calling the shots. Of course you're confused; of course you're freaking out. But you should also be excited to get started! It's your time to shine, to dig deep and discover who you are. This is the first time you're going to be making important choices not based on what your peers, your parents, or anyone else thinks or expects of you. *You* are in control.

Once I realized this, I felt completely empowered, and I was ready to face my future. I figured out a game plan, and I try to stick to it. Think about it like this: starting out is like being on a roller coaster. You know there are going to be some terrifying twists and turns, and you might feel scared or even sick to your stomach at times, but the thrill of the ride takes your breath away.

Buckle your seat belts . . . let's get started!

XOXO

whit

CHAPTER ONE

HOME SWEET HOME

For me, moving out was a huge step. It wasn't just about getting my own space and decorating it. My home was going to be a place I could call my own and be myself, a space where I could decompress after a hectic day and shed the layers. Emotionally, it meant I was breaking away from my parents, following my calling, and establishing what my life was really going to be about. I did a lot of talking about how I was an adult, but I didn't fully feel like one until I was out from under my parents' roof. College was the first time I had my own apartment, but it was still part of a safe community, with rules and boundaries and support.

My first apartment left a lot to be desired. It was dark and had the closet space of a Barbie town house; if I wore my four-inch stilettos and put my hair up, my head practically brushed the ceiling. It was far from a glamorous abode, but with a little ingenuity (and a whole lot of creativity), I transformed it into a space I was proud to call home—and wouldn't be mortified to have friends and family visit.

I tackled my decorating much in the same way I would approach putting together a great fashion ensemble: I mixed a little bit of this with a little bit of that, paired comfy classics with vintage or thrift-shop steals, and spiced it up with some color and bold accents. I am even known to use my own accessories like headbands and necklaces as interior design pieces. And, of course, I made sure to "Whitneyfy" it! I love to mix and match patterns; it's my funky twist on being eclectic. I really love an Art Deco kind of look that blends vintage and modern. *Architectural Digest* might never consider my apartment cover material, but that's okay. I loved how I made it my own on my budget.

IT'S ALL ABOUT YOU

Here's your opportunity to finally make your living space all your own. Own your identity! For your whole life, you've lived in a home filled with someone else's vision. You can finally let that inner interior designer out and make it as simplistic or ornate as you wish. Every square inch should reflect your personality, your taste, your essence. Yes, you want guests to ooh and aah when they come over. But frankly, you have to live here. Every day, every night. You have to feel comfortable; you have to feel inspired, relaxed, rejuvenated. Sure, white carpeting might look cool—but *hello*? Who's gonna clean it every time you track in some dirt on your shoes? I purposely chose a dark brown carpeting for this reason—one of my pet peeves is dirty carpet.

Take a good look around you—try to see the possibilities, not the problems. Don't just dwell on what your new dwelling is lacking (windows, closets, a corner of wall that is not peeling . . .). Instead, focus on the positives (It's cute and cozy!

This is my first New York City apartment in the Flatiron District. I loved the floor-to-ceiling windows and the views—although it certainly looked bare before I decorated!

The fridge and oven work! There's a pizza joint that delivers 24/7 down the block!). Like I said, my first place was no palace. I knew there was a ton to be done. But the idea of transforming something is exciting. You're doing your own *Extreme Home Makeover!*

At first, I bought things based on aesthetics. But then I quickly realized that although that's fun, and it's very easy to get carried away if something catches your eye, function and form really count. You should be able to collapse on your couch and put your feet up at the end of the day without worrying about ruining anything. So by all

You have to feel comfortable; you have to feel inspired, relaxed, rejuvenated.

means, buy pieces that "speak" to you—but just make sure they're usable as well.

I did a lot of thinking before I started decorating. I made a list (I make lots of lists—they're my secret weapon!). I knew what I needed: some creative ways to brighten things up and create the illusion of light and airiness. I wanted color. I am a California girl at heart, even if I am living in the heart of NYC. Dreary, dark, and

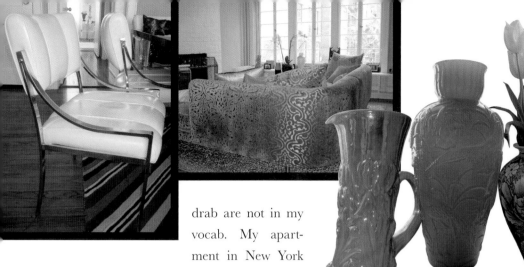

drab are not in my vocab. My apartment in New York could technically be considered a rainbow: my dining room table sits on top of a multicolor-striped carpet; I have a blue, purple, and green floral chair in my living room, and vases of every color. Plus, my bedroom is painted lavender . . . and my bed is black and white!

Think about everything you want your home to embody. What are the words you want to use to describe your dream dwelling? Cozy and comfy? Chic and sleek? Functional? Funky? Keep those words in mind as you shop. And remember, patience is a virtue. Rome wasn't built in a day; likewise, your first apartment. It takes some time (maybe even an eternity) to fully decorate your space. And just when you think you're totally done . . . you change your mind and redo everything to create a new vibe, or you move out! Go ahead—have fun furnishing. That's the best part of having your own home: no one is going to tell you that chintz

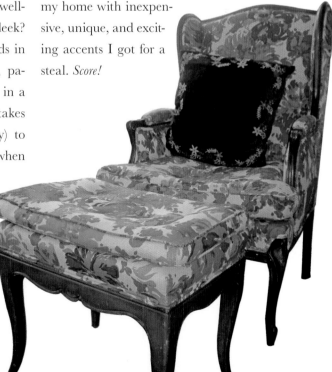

and plaid clash or that old 45s are not artwork.

And if you don't have a lot of money to decorate, no problem. Most of my favorite furnishings cost me next to nothing. You know that feeling when you find a stunning pair of shoes on the sale rack in your size? That's how I felt filling my home with inexpensive, unique, and exciting accents I got for a steal. *Score!*

DECORATING ON A BUDGET

No funds to furnish? Never fear, dear . . .

- **Somebody's trash can be** someone else's treasure. In every town there are countless thrift shops, flea markets, or yard/garage sales. Vintage pieces are some of the best finds I have. I nabbed my white leather dining room chairs at the thrift shop right next to my building in New York, as well as a colorful, floral-patterned comfy chair for my living room. I also go to Missouri every summer and browse the antique shops with my mom—that's where I pick up most of my lamps and vases. If I see something I like, I haggle! I will drive an hour outside town to this farmhouse that auctions everything off—from dish sets to bicycles, board games to John Deeres! It's a blast, and some of my favorite pieces come from these trips.

At seven years old with my two grandmothers: on the right is Grandma Nana, Dad's mama, and on the left is Grandma Bucka, Mom's mom.

It may sound gross, but this chair was actually left in my apartment by my predecessors.

- **Swapping furniture and home accessories** with friends is a great way to get rid of your clutter while also bringing new life into your space. Compile what you are willing to give up, then get together and do some fair trading!

- **Search a family member's garage or basement.** My grandmother is a huge collector of antiques, and over the years I have taken/been given vases, tea sets, lamps, candy dishes. My apartment has benefited from Gram's great finds!

- **Bright and bold colors** add drama where you want it; cool pastels soothe and calm. Slapping on a fresh coat of paint is a quick and easy fix. And I don't just mean the walls; don't be afraid to take a spray can to a dull piece of furniture to spruce it up.

- **Wallpaper is another great option;** anthropologie.com has some cool, unusual patterns—paper that looks like lace, letters, even silverware! Or, if you're artistically inclined, turn your walls into your own personal canvas. In my old college apartment, I would just take a marker to the wall and start doodling a design. If you—or anyone you know—has artistic ability, this is a great way to add bursts of color and whimsy to plain walls. Another trick I love: putting up bright swatches of fabric using pushpins. They won't damage the walls if you're worried about your landlord, and you can change the fabric to suit any mood or occasion.

I found this beautiful antique bar set in Osage Beach, too!

- **Can't afford new furniture?**
  Some inexpensive accessories can transform old pieces. Brighten up your old couch with funky pillows or a snazzy throw, and your ratty sofa is suddenly transformed! Need extra seats for entertaining? My best friend from childhood, Joanna Scapa, creatively scattered multicolored cushions around her living room floor. Practical *and* cool!

- **Camouflage floor or carpet**
  stains by throwing down some rug remnants. Mix colors, textures, even shapes. I even found a fab fake white fur rug at Costco!

- **Spruce up a boring bathroom**
  with a new shower curtain, some vibrant hand towels, and bath accessories. All can be found for cheap at places like Bed Bath and Beyond, Anthropologie, or Urban Outfitters, and they really make a difference. I'm also a huge fan of the Simply Shabby Chic for Target line. The white damask bathroom accessories feel pretty and feminine and cost under $20! You can even buy online!

- **Framed personal photos** make any space more special. I like to buy cheap frames and embellish them (you can hot-glue on gems, beach glass, shells, wine corks, buttons . . . just refrain from elbow macaroni, unless you're going for that elementary school look). You can also pull pages out of a vintage book or magazine and put them up in ready-made matted frames. Instant art collection! My favorite source for old books is the Strand in Union Square in NYC—but any used bookshop will have great options, or check out cheap-books.com or half.com. Sometimes, you can pick up dozens of books for less than a dollar each! I just snatch up a batch with colorful covers or spines, not even looking at the titles, and scatter them on shelves and tabletops to add some interest to the room.

- **Simple window treatments** instantly make a room look more luxe. You can pick up some inexpensive curtains or swags of fabric and hang them wherever you need a bit of color. Or if you know how to sew, buy some pretty fabric and hem it to hang on a rod. Suddenly, those plain white walls of your living room come to life!

- **Chalkboard paint can turn a wall or a portion of a wall into a full-on chalkboard.** You can keep a constant visual to-do list, visitors can draw and leave you messages, or you can go crazy and draw as you please. Get different-color chalk and go nuts!

- **Hit up your local fabric store** to re-cover a piece of furniture that has great bones but maybe needs a new vibe. Restain, re-paint, and re-cover. Voilà! Instant masterpiece. Usually re-covering a piece of furniture is cheaper and easier than buying some-thing completely new.

An antique find in Osage Beach, Missouri, where my family vacations.

YOUR CLOSET IS THE SIZE OF A SHOEBOX

I admit I am not the most organized person on the planet—probably because I spend a lot of time traveling and living out of suitcases (Excuses! Excuses!). But I do use every inch—and I mean every inch—of my space. I like to put space dividers in my drawers so I can separate out my undies, socks, tights, and bras. I also create categories in my closet: pants are hung together; likewise jackets, shirts, dresses, and skirts. And each category gets a different color hanger—so I can grab for red and know that the mini skirt I need is right there. And I do have one golden rule: put things away. That means no tossing stuff any which way into drawers (resulting in a future game of hide-and-seek), no piling clothes to the ceiling or leaving them on the floor. My mom always told me it takes just as little time to hang something up as it does to throw it on the floor. So true! And I'm much happier when my bedroom doesn't look like a tornado hit it.

There are many affordable and easy ways to store your stuff. Places like the Container Store, Target, Walmart, Bed

I'm much happier when my bedroom doesn't look like a tornado hit it.

Bath and Beyond, and so on, have amazingly cheap products that will help you maximize and compartmentalize.

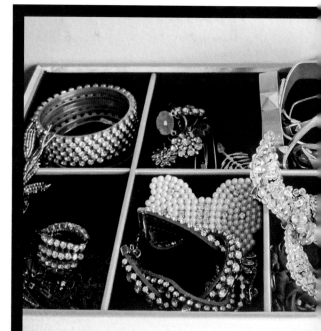

- **Risers for your bed are a great option** because they create a whole new storage space. You can store your winter clothes in summer and vice versa. Invest in some under-the-bed storage boxes or bags. The ones that vacuum-seal your sweaters flat are especially great for tight spaces.

- **Get the skinniest hangers you can;** the skinnier the hangers, the more of them you can have! If you're superpressed for space, use multitiered hangers to group skirts and pants together, or a rod that hangs from an existing one to create double the rack room.

- **Rotate seasonal clothes** front and center at eye level. For example, in the spring/summer, winter clothes should be placed out of ready-reach so your pretty sundresses are easy to find. Have

sweaters and coats laundered or dry-cleaned (be sure to empty all pockets) and consider storing them so you have more room.

- **Clip-on shelf dividers** are a great way to keep sweaters, hats, purses, shoes, and gloves separated and accessible. Or try using inexpensive wicker baskets on shelves or on the floor of your closet for storing accessories. A small towel rack hung on the inside of your closet door is perfect for keeping scarves tidy; a hanger with multiple three-ring-binder-type metal rings will hold belts and keep them in line.

- **Be creative with how you store your jewelry.** I have a small bowl next to my bed and I drop all the little things—like stud earrings and rings that I wear all the time—into it. I also have a mannequin in my apartment that I use to drape fabric, and she often gets adorned with my accessories. It's like a big paper doll! In my dresser, I have tons of boxes and trays of necklaces, earrings, and rings. Some other great ideas: use the necks of wine bottles to stack a collection of bangle bracelets; pick up an inexpensive tackle box and keep jewelry neat and tidy inside. I also love the idea of using an artist's wooden modeling hands to hold rings, bracelets, and so on. Whimsical and efficient!

- **Invest in instant "footwear files"** by buying a vertical shoe organizer; one that hangs over the back of the closet door will give you more room than one that sits on the closet floor—and it doesn't take up floor space. I categorize my shoes into boots, sandals, flats, close-toed heels, and open-toed heels and store them either on shelves or in an over-the-door rack. Sometimes, it simply helps to see what's inside the box. You can shoot Polaroids of your shoes and tape them to the boxes, or invest in see-through plastic boxes so you can find your mules in minutes.

- **I have tons of hair accessories** that can disappear if they're not well organized. I have a wrought-iron headband tree next to my bed. Bundles of barrettes? No prob. Clip them to a long ribbon (you can hang it up inside your closet door) so they won't wander away. Or simply tuck them in snack-size plastic bags, according to color or clip style, and store in a drawer.

LET THERE BE LIGHT!

A lot of apartments don't come with overhead lighting or even good natural light. In fact, my first two apartments didn't have any overhead lights at all. Good thing for me I love dim light—I think it's romantic and relaxing. But when you need to see and want to brighten up a dark room:

- **Keep walls and floors light;** it will instantly make the room look brighter and bigger. I love soft muted shades. In my first apartment, I did the living room in a light Tiffany blue color. In the bedroom of that apartment, I painted the wall behind my bed a dainty ballerina pink. Now my bedroom is a delicate lavender; it's so soothing. Lavender is one of my mom's fave colors, so when I am far away, it reminds me of her and home.

- **Forget dark furniture.** Go for warm, vibrant patterns on sofas and chairs. My couch is a turquoise paisley pattern. And try light-colored wood or white-finish furniture to brighten up the space and make it look bigger.

- **Wall sconces, table lamps, and floor lamps** that direct light up at the ceiling can help get rid of a cavelike atmosphere. Simple, cheap lamps are always easy to find either at Walmart, Target, ZGallerie. com, or a thrift shop; and you can customize them with spray paint and new shades. I have actually accessorized some of my lamp shades with brooches, pins, and earrings to add a funky element to a simple shade.

- **Mirrors give the illusion of light** because they reflect it. They open up a room, virtually "doubling" it in size. Place a mirror on a wall opposite a set of windows and suddenly you have tons of natural light. Standing mirrors are also a great fix; they give the optical illusion of a bigger room.

- **Candles, candles, candles . . .** beyond adding twinkling light to the darkest atmosphere, they smell heavenly.

- **Get rid of old fluorescent bulbs** and replace them with soft white incandescent bulbs that will make the lighting seem more natural. Or try full-spectrum bulbs, which cost a bit more than regular incandescent bulbs, but which mimic the sun's natural light.

This hand-painted candle is one of my favorites! It features gorgeous peonies (my favorite flower) in bright colors, and smells like them, too. I got it from gracioushome. com—an amazing place for home furnishings and accessories.

YOUR BEDROOM IS YOUR OASIS

The room you sleep in should be a sexy, spiritual haven. Bad day at work, be gone! Nothing can bother me when I'm snuggled in my bed. Your bedroom is a place for you to escape and cocoon. My one hard-and-fast rule: I never bring my laptop into bed. Your bedroom should never be associated with work (only play!). My bedroom is lavender, with a black-and-white-patterned headboard (which was an antique room divider that my mom found), cream-colored bedding with hints of black and silver, a soft, white faux fur rug, lots of eclectic picture frames, and a floor mirror that has mother-of-pearl edging. I do basically *everything* in my bedroom: watch TV, read magazines, eat popcorn in bed (bad habit), dance around to music, put on my makeup, and style my hair. Even if you're in a studio apartment—and your bed is literally part of your living room—little touches can help you unwind and de-stress:

- **Your bed is your best friend** at the end of a long day. Invest in your comfort by purchasing a feather bed (it sits on top of the mattress giving it extra softness) and a plush down (or down-alternative) comforter. I went to Bloomingdale's with my mom to try it all out. In my opinion, thick and cushiony is the way to go. There is just nothing like sinking into a soft cloud. *Ahhh . . .*

- **Itchy sheets are a no-no.** If you can't afford a high thread count, do what I do: buy sheets in super-soft jersey T-shirt material. I love Pure Beech sheets at Bed Bath and Beyond. They come in every color imaginable and are as soft as a twenty-year-old T-shirt.

- **Have a plethora of pillows.** I sleep with four: two are in the tee material, two are in ultrasoft

Step into my boudoir . . . My cozy bed has lots
of pillows, and extra blankets for extra comfort.

fleece. They remind me of comfy, fuzzy socks. Heaven! Thus two of the pillows are cold when I get in bed and two are warm. I know, I'm weird!

- **Scent your room.** Candles and reed diffusers fill your entire space with fragrance and are inexpensive. They help to set the mood for relaxing on a Sunday morning or help energize me for a night out. You can even go online and make your own scent at reeddiffusers.org. I love the scent of peonies and gardenias. One of my fave candles is by Votivo in "Clean, Crisp White." It smells like fresh laundry! I also love the scent of vanilla, peony, and anything by Diptyque.

- **Fill your room with fresh flowers or plants.** Pick them from outside or find a cheap bunch at the market; they put a smile on my face whenever I smell or see them. Lily of the valley, lavender, roses, narcissus, and lilacs are particularly fragrant. Roxy was staying at my apartment this weekend while I was away, and as a thank-you, she put a vase of peach roses next to my bed with a note. When I got home, it was like walking into a room filled with sunshine!

- **I live in my blanket** when I am in the comfort of my bedroom. Try to find a fleece fabric; you will never want to take it off. I just wrap it around myself. The ultimate Snuggie! When I'm home in L.A., my family makes fun of me for stealing all the blankets and wearing them around the house.

- **Are you a light person . . . or a dark one?** I personally love sunlight and moonlight streaming through my windows. If that's the case for you, choose gauzy, sheer curtains. They'll be cooler in the summer, too, allowing the breeze to stream in. If you must have total darkness to slumber, then invest in blackout shades (and a great sleep mask).

- **Decorate your bedroom with photos.** My mom hung pictures with clothespins on a clothesline in my sister's dorm room so that she could display all of her pictures without taking up too much space. It made my sister feel happy and at home—even when she was at college. Likewise, every ledge and tabletop in my apartment holds frames with pictures of my friends, family, and special occasions. If you've got too many photos to display individually, you can pick up a plain corkboard, wrap it in ribbon or fabric, and create your own memory board. Or pick up a digital frame with a large memory stick; this can hold hundreds of images! Scrapbooks are also fun, personal coffee-table books. I have scrapbooks from my friend Christina from college and my best friend, Andrea, as books on my living-room coffee table.

- **Color your room cozy.**
Paint colors that are too bold or dark can be a distraction in your bedroom. They also make the space feel a lot smaller than it is. If you want to feel relaxed and peaceful, be sure that the color on the walls is neutral or pastel such as tan, cream, light blue, light pink, and light yellow. Avoid harsh colors like red, black, and dark green. Your bedding can be bolder, but keep it in the same color family; clashing colors will not soothe the nerves. Personally, I like more neutral, muted tones for the bed, shades of white, cream, nude, and pastels. But you should do what works for you.

- **I am all about texture: soft, fluffy, or floaty fabrics** that feel nice to the touch. You can mix and match them; shag rugs with flannel bedding; satin pillows with cotton sheets; a crocheted throw or cashmere-blend blankets over a silky duvet.

- **Bedroom lighting should be soft, calm, romantic.** No bright, blaring overheads. Fluorescent lighting is my ultimate nightmare. I'd rather shower or get ready in the dark with light from one candle than function under fluorescent. Think dim and delicate for drowsing. I also love candlelight in my bedroom. There's something about the soft flicker of the flame that lulls me to sleep.

STOCKING UP: WHAT EVERY GIRL NEEDS IN HER . . .

Stocking up is more than just filling your shelves, cabinets, or drawers with "stuff." It empowers you by helping you feel prepared for whatever comes your way. I may not be emotionally prepared for every scenario, but at least I know I have the right supplies to handle the situation—be it a flashlight, extra batteries, or some cough medicine. There's also something very "grown up" about planning for the future, and not just "winging it."

When I felt a cold coming on recently, and my mom called to ask if I had everything I needed, I was proud to say, "Yup, I've got it all under control." And I wasn't just saying that: prewinter, I filled my medicine cabinet with cold and flu essentials, so if I was alone and feeling crappy, I didn't have to crawl out to the drugstore to get medicine. I still felt stuffy headed and sniffly for a few days, but I reveled in my independence!

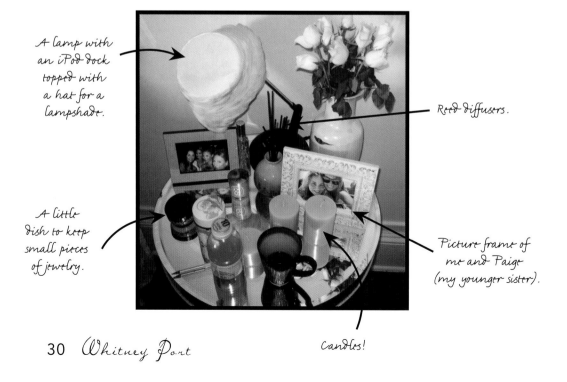

A lamp with an iPod dock topped with a hat for a lampshade.

Reed diffusers.

A little dish to keep small pieces of jewelry.

Picture frame of me and Paige (my younger sister).

Candles!

Nightstand Drawer

An essential next to your bed is a good moisturizing hand cream (if you have it handy, you'll use it)—my new fave is called Breathe by Lollia (Lollialife.com), which I found at Anthropologie. You should also have in your nightstand drawer: a condom (if you have it handy, you'll use it!); a good book or your Kindle/iPad; a flashlight; lip moisturizer, makeup-removing towelettes (in case you're too lazy to walk to the bathroom to take off your makeup—it happens to all of us); gum or mints (good as you are putting your purse together to walk out the door) or some gummy candies for late-night snacking; tissues.

Medicine Cabinet

Here you should store your meds (throw out all prescriptions that have expired), Band-Aids in assorted sizes, gauze, antiseptics such as alcohol and hydrogen peroxide for cleansing cuts or scrapes, an antibiotic cream, a salve for minor burns, an anesthetic spray for sunburns, aloe vera, over-the-counter antihistamine for allergic reactions, a cortisone-based topical cream, over-the-counter pain medications, a cough suppressant/expectorant, a cold medication, and a sore throat spray or nose spray for congestion. You might also want to have a sunscreen and a bug spray on hand—especially during the summer—lip balm, tweezers (for eyebrows as well as splinters), and eyedrops.

Bookshelf

Obviously, you should stock your shelves with books you love, even if they're old faves from childhood (Go on! Proudly display your Judy Blume or Nancy Drew collection!), college classics, or just fun, "escape." I keep all of my fashion magazines on my bookshelves—every single issue of *Vogue, Bazaar,* and *Elle* since I've been living in NYC. I draw inspiration from them. When I'm stumped on a design or an outfit, or need hairstyle or makeup ideas, I thumb through the pages to revisit fashion seasons past. It's also important to have reference books handy, like a thesaurus and a dictionary, and some books relevant to your job or field (in my case, fashion). And collect a few photo or coffee-table books about beautiful places, people, or things—eye candy that you or your guests can browse.

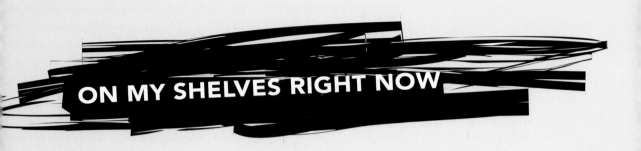

ON MY SHELVES RIGHT NOW

Are You There, Vodka? It's Me, Chelsea by Chelsea Handler

Chanel and Her World by Edmonde Charles-Roux

Diane: A Signature Life by Diane von Furstenberg

The Fashion Designer Survival Guide by Mary Gehlhar

The Great Gatsby by F. Scott Fitzgerald

If You Have to Cry, Go Outside:
  And Other Things Your Mother Never Told You by Kelly Cutrone

Images of Marilyn from Parragon Books

L.A. Candy and *Sweet Little Lies* by Lauren Conrad

Mario Testino: Portraits by Mario Testino

Patrick Demarchelier by Patrick Demarchelier

Poseur by Rachel Maude

Prince of Tides by Pat Conroy

Shabby Chic Interiors by Rachel Ashwell

The *Twilight* Saga by Stephenie Meyer

Valentino: Themes and Variations by Valentino and Pamela Golbin

The Way We Live in the City by Stafford Cliff and Gilles de Chabeneix

Yves Saint Laurent's Style by Foundation Pierre Bergé

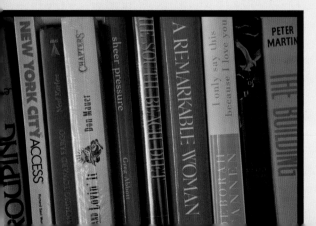

DVD Collection

Build a collection of movies from different genres and times, including some tearjerkers, powerhouse dramas, sweeping romances, or even zany comedies. That way, if you have friends over, you have films that appeal to everyone (and you're not scrambling to get to Blockbuster!). I also keep on hand movies that *always* make me laugh and cry or remind me of specific eras in my life (like college or high school). I probably have watched them more than a dozen times each, but I never get tired of them. In fact, I know a lot of the lines by heart: "Isn't my house classic? The columns date all the way back to 1972!" (Alicia Silverstone in *Clueless*).

MY MOVIE MUST-HAVES

Clueless

Elizabethtown

Fast Times at Ridgemont High

Father of the Bride

Forever Young

Forrest Gump

A League of Their Own

Legends of the Fall

Love, Actually

Mermaids

Motorcycle Diaries

My Father the Hero

New York Minute

Now and Then

Pretty Woman

Pursuit of Happyness

Shakespeare in Love

Stand by Me

Teen Witch

When Harry Met Sally

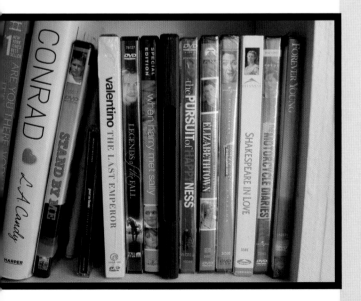

Fridge/Pantry

Basically, you want to cram your kitchen with healthy essentials you will eat every day. For me, that's Granny Smith apples and bananas with freshly churned peanut butter, berries and Reddi-wip, whole-grain English muffins, Parmesan cheese, avocados, almond milk, nonfat Greek yogurt, vegetables to roast, unsalted butter, whole-wheat bread, roasted and unsalted almonds, veggie burgers, cherry tomatoes, Raisin Bran cereal, original Popchips, rice cracker mix, artichokes, plums, and greens. I know other people make and freeze tons of meals ahead of time and their fridges are overflowing with yummy dishes. If you have the time (and the know-how) to cook, that's great. If you're not as culinarily inclined, like me, keep it simple. Make sure you have healthy choices in there that will work for breakfast, lunch, and dinner . . . and everything in between. And keep some backup snack foods on hand in case a friend drops by or you invite a few coworkers back after an event.

A few healthy suggestions (my faves!):

- Fresh vegetables: artichokes, broccoli, cauliflower, brussels sprouts, butternut squash, mushrooms
- Fresh fruit: Granny Smith apples, bananas, papaya, strawberries, pineapple, plums
- Dried fruit: mango, apricots, Craisins
- Frozen fruits: strawberries, blueberries, raspberries
- Salsa: Homemade is always best! I chop tomatoes and onions and add salt, pepper, and a dash of cilantro

- Peanut butter and jelly: My fave PB is fresh churned from Whole Foods
- Almond milk
- Whole grains: bread (love La Brea Bakery bread), pita, brown rice, cereal, healthy crackers, Pop-chips, red quinoa
- Low-fat microwavable popcorn
- Edamame
- Parmesan chunks with almonds
- Trail mix

Emergency Supplies

Keep these somewhere handy—like a kitchen drawer (not buried in the back of your closet!): a flashlight, batteries, emergency phone numbers, spare set of keys to your home, bottles of water, scissors, screwdrivers (Phillips and flat head) and hammer, candles and matches, transistor radio.

SAFETY SMARTS

Ladies, living alone can be scary—and it goes without saying that you should take a few precautions. In college, I had an experience that creeped me out and taught me something about security. I had this stupid habit of not locking my apartment door. Well, one night, a guy wandered in and got into bed with me! I was freaking out, but tried to sound calm and polite. I said, "Excuse me? Excuse me!" hoping he would take the hint and get out from under my blankets. I later found out he was one of the guys from a neighboring unit. Thankfully, he didn't mean any harm—he just was so wasted, he thought he was in his own bed.

But this unwanted visitor made me think twice about how secure I was in my space. To this day, my mind plays tricks on me. I hear creaking floors and I jump a mile. Probably for this reason, my mom made me get one of those high-tech security systems as well as a second lock. At first, I thought she was being overprotective. But I realize it does help me sleep better at night (my place is locked up tighter than Fort Knox!). I think anytime you're proactive, you feel *much* better. You don't want to be paranoid, but you also don't want to be naive. Here are a few recommendations from the NYPD Crime Prevention Unit that make a lot of sense:

- **If you're coming and going at odd hours** (early in the morning/late at night), and your place doesn't have a doorman or security camera, have someone watch until you get in your door (dates don't seem to mind this . . . it could mean a good-night kiss at the door). Never walk alone past 10:00 P.M.! My mom gets so mad at me if she finds out I was strolling solo past this time. It's like an indirect curfew placed from over three thousand miles away, but it keeps me safe.

- **If you are coming home alone,** double-check that no one is lurking around. Carry your keys in your hand so you can immediately get inside and lock the door behind you. Digging around in the bottom of your bag can allow someone to sneak up behind you. Your keys can also be used as a defensive weapon if someone attacks you. And shut the door right away—do not let it close on its own.

- **Always carry a cell phone!** Carry a personal alarm in your purse. Some come on a key chain and make a loud, piercing sound; others will even dial 911.

- **Avoid places like stairwells,** laundry rooms, and parking lots late at night. There is no reason to be at those places after hours.

- **Make sure the hallway** outside your door is brightly lit. If not, speak to your landlord.

- **Double-check that your windows and doors are locked** securely when you're in and when you're out; you may also want a safety chain or a deadbolt and bars on your windows. The first thing one of my friends bought for her new apartment was a little dog with a big bark! It's like having an alarm system on legs . . .

- **Don't give a lot of people** copies of your keys. And don't leave a spare lying around under your doormat, in a flowerpot, in a mailbox, or in other obvious places. If you tend to lose your keys often, give *one* set to a trusted neighbor or friend.

- **Don't "announce" to everyone that you're a young woman living on your own.** In fact, when you record the message on your home phone, have a guy friend or your dad do it . . . or say "WE can't come to the phone right now . . ." When I moved to NYC, I took my brother's old phone, and his voice still picks up on the answering machine. I've never changed it.

- **Take a woman's personal safety/self-defense class.** It can give you peace of mind, and a lot of police precincts, community colleges, and local Ys offer them for free or for a small fee. Krav Maga is a great one. You'll learn what to watch out for and how to protect yourself in an emergency.

CHAPTER TWO

WORKING

GIRL

Job interviews are agonizing enough—try doing one while cameras are filming you! In 2005, I was going to USC and working as an intern at *Women's Wear Daily* in L.A. It was in the same building as *Teen Vogue*, and I heard they were looking for interns as well. I jumped at the opportunity and quickly sent in my résumé. I soon got an invitation to meet with their fashion editorial team. *Gulp.* During the course of the interview, they asked me lots of questions—many of which I was painfully unprepared to answer. I didn't know the names of some of the key editors on staff; I hadn't heard of many of the important photographers they used. I thought I blew it. Then came the strangest question of all, "We've been approached by MTV for a reality TV show. How would you feel about being on camera?"

I didn't really feel anything; I had no idea what this would entail. Seriously . . . I just wanted the job at *Teen Vogue*! I agreed to do a casting tape for MTV, which I thought went a little smoother (they didn't ask me the names of any of *their* staff!). A month later, I was called back to *Teen Vogue*—this time to meet with Lisa Love, the West Coast fashion editor. Don't let her last name fool you; Lisa has a really tough reputation (though she still has a lot of love to give). I knew she would put me to the test. And I was warned that MTV was shooting the whole thing. If I was nervous before, now I was a wreck.

I wanted the job so much I could taste it. It was a great opportunity to make my

I wanted the job so much I could taste it.

next move in fashion and *Vogue*—come on, that's the dream! But I also knew I wasn't the only one: when I arrived for the interview, the lobby was filled with eager young hopefuls, all just as qualified—if not more so—as I was. Part of my brain was screaming "Make a run for it!" but I took a deep breath and sunk quietly into a seat. I sat there waiting, waiting, waiting to be called in, and eyeing all the competition.

It was a very formal reception area with a big marble desk, comfy chairs, and big posters of all the current Condé Nast covers. The girls and guys interviewing for a position were all superstylish in sophisticated knee-length skirts or trousers and collared

Where would I be without those ladies? Left, with Rox and Kelly; right, Lauren and me.

blouses or shirts and ties. None of them seemed to be as jittery as I was. Or maybe they were just better at hiding it.

We chatted and compared experiences, and it made me feel even more insecure; they all seemed so qualified, cool, and confident. Then Lauren Conrad from *Laguna Beach* walked in. Her hair was flat-ironed straight, and she was wearing a tailored blouse, a dark pencil skirt, and high heels. The girl looked so put together and profes-

sional (even though I later learned she had ten minutes to change and get down there!). How would I stand a chance against *her*? I looked down at my outfit. I *thought* I looked cute when I left the house: I was wearing a vintage collared beige blouse and *jeans*. What was I thinking? And as if that wasn't bad enough, I rounded out the outfit with Frye boots. Yikes! But I was holding in my hands a printed résumé when a lot of the girls and guys didn't have theirs—so hopefully that earned me brownie points for being prepared.

Lucky for me, Lisa Love and the rest of the staff at *Teen Vogue* saw beyond my bad fashion choices. I think my passion and drive to learn convinced them I wasn't a total disaster. I got the job, and Lauren (she was also hired as a fashion department intern) and I, of course, became good friends. But I learned a lot about what to do—and not to do—on an interview and in the workplace.

THE JOB INTERVIEW

So here's the good news: if you're called for an interview, the employer thinks you potentially have what it takes. You look great on paper; now comes your chance to show what you've got and prove you're as fabulous as your cover letter claims. The goal of the interview is not just to see if you're the real deal; it's also to evaluate if you and the company "mesh." The interviewer wants to make sure you're a good fit to work here. You want to be yourself in any interview, but you also want to show that you are capable of adapting to any work environment with enthusiasm, that you will have respect for your fellow staffers, and that you possess ingenuity. Every workplace is unique, and of course, it's the sum of its parts. It's the people who make up the company as much as it is the product/service that's offered. So the interviewer needs to see that you're going to be comfortable and make those around you comfortable as well.

Put on a happy face.

Seriously. Do not come in looking like you've just lost your best friend or your cell phone on the bus. Worry shows; wipe it from your face and flash a dazzling smile as you firmly shake the interviewer's hand (I did say firm; not a vicelike grip!). A handshake is underrated. My dad has judged many a man who has walked through our front door based on his grip! Tell yourself you're going to be positive and optimistic; practice thinking happy thoughts: "I will get this job. I am a great catch for any company!" So when you walk in and see that interviewer for the first time, you project confidence, charisma, and a coolness that only someone sincerely wonderful could possess. This is not faking it; this is making it happen!

Follow his/her lead.

If the interviewer engages in small talk ("Crazy weather we're having!" "Love your shoes!"), then by all means relax and chat right back. Be appropriate, yes, but also realize he/she may be trying to put you at ease or gauge how much of a "people person" you are. If your answers are only monosyllabic, you won't allow the interviewer to get a feel for how you communicate. Expect the unexpected. A friend of mine went into a serious interview at an investment bank, expecting to be quizzed about the state of the economy and Wall Street. Instead, the interviewer wanted to know (since my friend mentioned on her résumé she had briefly studied in Italy) if she had been to Voltera where they shot the *New Moon* movie. They spent an hour gabbing about their mutual passion for *Twilight* and RPattz; not a word about finance was uttered. And guess what? She got the job on the spot!

Then there was Roxy. I know she might have come off a little abrasive in her interview with notoriously tough Kelly Cutrone at People's Revolution, but really, she was riffing off Kelly's vibe. Pretty ingenious: she was trying to show Kelly she was a lot like her (attitude and all!).

Make yourself perfectly clear.

That means make sure you say what you mean and that you speak loud enough and articulate (no mumbling!) so the interviewer understands you. Think before you

Tell yourself you're going to be positive and optimistic. This is not faking it; this is making it happen!

open your mouth; listen carefully to what he/she has just asked you. If you don't understand the question, ask the interviewer to repeat it ("Excuse me? Can you repeat that?"). Or better yet, say the question in your own words and ask the interviewer to confirm that you understood properly. I'm not afraid to say, "That's a really difficult question . . ." and then take a deep breath and think it through. I try not to blurt something out without processing it.

Sometimes an interviewer might even say something you don't agree with. When this happens to me, I try to be rational and levelheaded. My mom always told me to validate someone's feelings, then in a polite way state my opinion. So I'll say "I hear you" or "Fair enough," then explain my take on it. Sometimes people respect when their authority is questioned and you prove you have a strong viewpoint.

What if you're still stumped? Think about what the interviewer would want/ expect you to say—and what the *true* purpose of the question is. For example, on an interview at Bergdorf's when I was showing my clothing line, the buyer asked me what I thought of a certain fabric on one of my samples. I loved this fabric, but I could tell she was fishing for something (and potentially hated it). So I explained why I thought it was the perfect material for a dress: comfy, forgiving of any figure flaws, and it had a touch of sparkle to it, which made it ideal for transforming quickly from a day to evening look. She was satisfied with my response, even if she didn't flip over my fabric choice. Why? Because I allowed her to see my thought process when creating my line. Her question really had a secret underlying question: "Whitney, how do you design?"

Ask away!

The best way to convey you're eager to join the team (without getting up on the desk and doing a cheer) is to ask relevant and intelligent questions. I'm not talking about "So how long do we get for lunch?" or "What's your policy on sick days?" or even "Do we get year-end bonuses?" or "Is there a free dress day?" Even if these questions are burning in your mind, stick to the topics you know the interviewer would like to hear about: "What is the company's goal for the upcoming year?" "What would my role be and what would a typical day be like for me?" As you leave, give the interviewer a firm handshake and thank him/her for meeting with you. Make sure to show a lot of interest in the company—people love curiosity.

Just a few things to keep in mind (I hope these go without saying . . . but I gotta say them):

- No cleavage.
- No microminis.
- No Moon Boots or sky-high platforms.
- No skintight leather.
- No going commando; undies are a must!
- No ripped, tattered, or stained clothing (even if you've patched it).
- No bra straps, panty lines, or belly-button piercings on display.
- No tees with offensive slogans. Roxy recently wore a shirt to *Glamour*'s offices that said the "F" word. The editors were in shock (and I was a little embarrassed)!

A pencil skirt is a sophisticated cut, but this fabric is metallic and playful.

This outfit is demure but still fashion-forward with puffy sleeves and stripes. It mixes edge with femininity.

EATING ON THE JOB

Part of succeeding at work is making sure you have the tools you need—and that includes the right snacks to stay focused and healthy. When you feel the

midday brain drain, scarfing down some candy from the vending machine—or making a run to the coffee store for an iced mocha something—sounds very tempting. When you're tired and stressed at work, it's hard to resist a little pick-me-up. Sugar and caffeine offer instant gratification. But guess what? Less than an hour later, the euphoria has worn off, and you're even more tired than before.

There are smart ways to snack. When I know I am going to have a busy day—and have no idea where or when my next meal will be—I pack a bunch of snacks such as fruit leather, dried fruit, or a banana. I slice a Granny Smith apple and put a spoonful of peanut butter in a Tupperware container. Or I pack a baggie of popcorn to pop in the office micro, a handful of almonds, maybe a Fiber One bar and a Vitaminwater. It's a good idea to eat something that contains both protein and carbs; this will help maintain your blood-sugar level for the rest of the afternoon and stave off your hunger until the next meal. Some other good snacks to keep handy:

Nuts.

They provide healthy fats along with fiber—so you stay fuller longer. Buy a bunch of different unsalted varieties and make your own trail mix.

Hummus.

This is a low-glycemic-index food. Translation: These foods release their energy slowly, so you won't feel that dreaded blood-sugar spike after you refuel. Try two table-spoons of hummus with ten baby carrots. It's only about a hundred calories!

A sweet potato.

Pop one in the microwave and you'll instantly erase your sugar craving (and fill up on fiber). Fill with a little salt, pepper, olive oil, and Girard's light champagne dressing.

Edamame.

Soy beans are a vegetable loaded with protein. Microwave them, add a little salt, and you're set. Pair them with some Wheat Thins and you're good to go!

DAY TO NIGHT: HOW TO TRANSFORM YOUR WORK ATTIRE TO ON-THE-TOWN CHIC

Some days you are *so* busy, you just won't have the opportunity to go home and change before going out. This happens to me all the time, so I've become quite the "quick-change artist." I can get ready for a date or a girls' night out with lightning speed. It's simple: I either add to or take off from my day look.

Here's how:

Start with a little black dress in silk, satin, velvet, chiffon, or even jersey knit.

The posh material screams "party." But when you wear it to work, topped with a simple blazer or cardigan, it's suddenly office appropriate. When it's time to go out, peel off the jacket or sweater and you're ready!

Accessorize!

The fastest way to dress up a simple sheath or suit is to add beautiful jewelry. I pile on bangles, chains, dangly earrings (you can store them in a zip bag in your purse). Or carry a glitzy evening bag or clutch (just tuck it in your tote). The touch of sparkle makes your outfit evening-ready instantly.

Swap your shoes.

Leave the loafers under your desk. A pair of sexy stilettos or ankle boots glams up even the most mundane office attire. I especially like to strap on a pair in gold or silver—or a bold color. Very flirty!

Change your do.

If you normally wear your hair up at the office, then let it down at night. Or if you like it loose for day, sweep it into a messy bun for evening. The idea is to do your do differently. You'll feel special and sexy. And confidence is the best accessory!

Makeup makeover.

Bring makeup remover towelettes and remove face makeup, then put on some tinted moisturizer, blush, and bronzer for an instant glow. Slick on a darker, more daring lipstick and smoky eyeliner for evening. They'll instantly make your face look more glam and refreshed. These wipes can double to wipe under your armpits. Always carry a little stick of deodorant to reapply. Don't forget to spritz on a little perfume, too. Scent invigorates!

WHITTYISM: HOW TO HIDE A HANGOVER AT WORK

One of the best parts of being a single gal in the city is staying out late (no curfews!) and partying with friends. The worst part: waking up on a weekday morning after I've danced till dawn and downed one too many glasses of champagne. Luckily, I've found a way to erase the effects of a hangover from hell before I hit the office! (Or at least I try.)

When You Get Home

- Always wash your face before going to bed or use Pond's, L'Oreal, or Comodynes Wet Cleansing Towelettes.
- Even if your head is pounding, try to brush your hair before going to bed. It will feel so good on your scalp! And even rub in some Moroccan oil as a conditioning agent.
- Run some Frédéric Fekkai Protein Rx Creme through your tresses, then twist them into a bun. You'll wake to pretty waves and volume.
- Smooth on eye cream and lip balm, and lots of face moisturizer.
- Chug water!

In the A.M.

- Drinking takes its toll on skin; alcohol will dry your face out like the Sahara. So spritz skin with a moisturizing spray (or in a pinch, plain, cool water) to give it a freshening wake-up call. Finer Skin Institute and Philosophy make great ones.
- Apply a rich, soothing moisturizer—preferably one with some built-in shimmer, like Fresh High Noon Freshface Glow tinted moisturizer—to brighten and replenish.
- Next, focus on the eyes—they're probably swollen, ringed with dark circles, and bloodshot. Rohto cooling eyedrops will instantly get the red out, and a soothing eye cream (look for ones that specifically cool and firm) is a must before applying concealer—otherwise known as a girl's best friend. I also put spoons in the freezer and then rest the backs of the spoons on my eyelids for fifteen minutes. Ahh . . . It really works!
- Finally, bring the glow back to your cheeks with a dot of rosy blush and bronzer such as Nars Orgasm and Nars Laguna. You want to add just a hint of color to your complexion—especially if you look green or pasty. Don't overdo it—a dead giveaway that you were out all night and are trying to hide the evidence.

EVIL COWORKERS

Honey, it happens . . . you suddenly realize you're being asked to work alongside Cruella De Vil. These toxic types abound in the workplace. I was shocked when at DVF, my colleague Olivia Palermo went from palling around to plotting against me in a matter of weeks. At first, I thought she was just a shallow society girl—haughty but harmless. I had a hunch that the producers picked her for *The City* because she was very outspoken; I didn't suspect she was also underhanded. When we were assigned to pull DVF clothes together for an upcoming Jessica Alba shoot, she was bossy and opinionated. She trashed every outfit I suggested and allowed only one—a cute floral jacket and shorts—to make it to the rack for the shoot. When my outfit was actually chosen for the cover, Olivia quickly took all the credit. I stood there, utterly dumbfounded as my boss, Alixe, patted her on the back, and Olivia, who was beaming, said, "Styling is my passion!"

In retrospect, I was just as much to blame as she was. I didn't speak up when my boss congratulated her for spearheading the project. I allowed myself to be a doormat. What was I thinking? I knew I had chosen that outfit, but I didn't take credit where credit was due. I didn't try to set the record straight. I guess I was a little intimidated—but also just utterly stunned that someone could be so ruthless. I am also someone who doesn't like conflict; I hate to make a scene. But in situations like this, when someone you work with is clearly lying, cheating, and trying to make you look like a loser, you have to stand up for yourself! I vented to my girlfriends about it—which made me feel better—but then I simply stood there *again* at a luncheon with Diane von Furstenberg and Joe Zee, the creative director of *Elle*, as Olivia told them all, "I pulled that look!" Such a lie!

Every time I tried to work with Olivia, it was the same story: she was dismissive, rolled her eyes, and acted as if I was an idiot when it came to fashion. What was *that* about? Well, it was meant to knock my confidence for a loop. I totally see that now: when someone is insecure about her own abilities, she tries to put you down to make herself feel bigger and better. Classic bully technique.

Of course—as anyone who's ever seen a Disney cartoon knows—the villain eventually gets her just deserts. I say *eventually*, because it may not happen for a long, long time and you may begin to think there is no justice in the universe! When we were doing a presentation of DVF handbags, I was a nervous wreck, and Olivia kept telling me she wasn't worried at all ("Easy! Piece of cake!"). Then she totally stuttered and stammered and lost it at the presentation. Redemption!

With Olivia Palermo at Bryant Park—I'm too excited for the Diane von Furstenberg show to worry about our dysfunctional relationship.

Even though we don't work together anymore, Olivia still knows how to push my buttons. She is now a journalist for Elle.com and she interviews up-and-coming designers (that would be me!). So we

I *so* wanted to tell her what I thought of her manipulative and mean-spirited tactics!

scheduled a photo shoot for the site, and she was all set to come and interview me about my Whitney Eve line. Well, true to form, she decided three hours into the shoot that she wasn't coming because she didn't want to "endorse" my line. She kept saying that she had personal issues she had to deal with, but I didn't buy it. It felt like once again, she was trying to put me down and make me look bad.

But did I let Olivia irritate me all over again? Well, maybe for a few minutes . . . but then I shrugged it off. When you have a coworker who gets on your nerves, you have to rise above. Do your best. Work your hardest. If you get caught up in all the toxic talk and mind games, you're going to wind up making *yourself* look bad (something she is trying so hard to do!). I *so* wanted to tell her what I thought of her manipulative and mean-spirited tactics! I wanted to shout, "Olivia, what is your problem?" or rat her out to our bosses. But my friends told me not to sink to her level, to not get caught up in the drama. Instead, they told me to just focus, be myself, be the bigger person. I think that's great advice. Eventually, in a very peaceful manner, I did give her a piece of my mind, but it served more as closure for me than as a lesson for her.

Here's some other ways to deal with divas at work:

Keep your cool.

As tempting as it may be to launch into a tirade (or give her the good spanking she deserves), remember you are in a professional workplace. You have to behave like a pro. Let her be the one to make a scene; try to keep cool, no matter how many buttons she pushes. One of my friends told me when she gets worked up at work, she pictures Glinda the Good Fairy from *The Wizard of Oz* leaning over her shoulder, waving her twinkling wand, and ridding the room of that wicked witch. Try it; you may just giggle at the thought, but it certainly will take your mind off the tension.

Don't share your personal biz.

When I was breaking up with Jay Lyon, I was really sad. Olivia asked me (pretending to be concerned) why I seemed so down. When I told her, she snapped, "You need to focus on your work, not your relationship. Don't bring him into the workplace. That's incredibly immature." So much for sympathy! But I laid myself open to it; I should *never* have shared private info with someone I know has it out for me.

Stay away from a showdown.

Olivia loved to lure me in to one-upmanship . . . like the time we went to meet Manolo Blahnik at Bergdorf's. I was so excited to be buying my first pair, and Olivia announced she not only owned several, but had since she was seventeen! Well, I couldn't top that one and I wasn't going to let her ruin my excitement. Instead of trying to one-up her, I just thought: *Okay, Olivia, you win.* It's a waste of energy to get into a game of "Anything you can do, I can do better." You can't waste your time constantly defending yourself to people who only try to bring you down because of their own insecurities.

CHAPTER THREE

STYLE

P art of becoming your own person is developing and owning your personal style. I like to think of it as getting into your fashion groove: what looks good; what feels good; what colors and styles are superflattering to your body and skin tone. It's all about *you*. If everyone wore the same style, we'd all look like those cookie-cutter chicks in the Robert Palmer videos. No two people are exactly alike, and your style should be as unique as you are.

But fashion can be intimidating: all those crazy couture looks on the runway, all the new trends and fads being touted in the fashion magazines. How do you know which ones will work for you—and which will make you look like Lady Gaga? How do you know what to buy and what you can even afford? When you're this confused and overwhelmed, it's much easier to just pull on the same pair of jeans and sneakers and call it a day. Like most subjects, style requires some study. Yes, you're out of college, but you still have some homework ahead of you.

Start with a stack of fashion magazines, like *Vogue, Elle, Harper's Bazaar, Glamour,* or *InStyle.* As you look at photos or ads, what colors catch your eye? What styles can you see yourself wearing with confidence? Don't get hung up on the fact that the people wearing these clothes may be thinner/taller/more endowed than you are. Trust me; few people in real life look like they regularly strut the catwalks.

If you love something, there is *always* a way to wear it. I draw inspiration from style.com, where I can watch all the runway

If you love something, there is *always* a way to wear it.

shows and how each look is styled. It's a great way to gauge what's "in fashion" and also figure out how everything works together. Another great site that sparks my creativity is whowhatwear.com.

Once you've done a little homework, start by pulling a few pieces out of your closet and putting them together in a way that gels with your new "vision." Maybe it's pairing a bold-colored accessory—like a belt, a hat, a bag, or shoes—with a neutral classic. Maybe it's mixing superfeminine pieces—like lacy camisoles or silky blouses—with something more casual, like jeans or even leather. Consider this: What do you want your style to say about you? It can be any-

thing from "I'm sophisticated and elegant" to "I'm funky and fun-loving." And don't think that you have to stick with this style if you suddenly feel inspired to change it. I am a bit of a fashion schizophrenic; I don't ever become married to one look for too long. It's more fun that way!

Inspiration board for Whitney Eve.

My messy closet!

MY FASHION EVOLUTION

Although I love Valentino and Zac Posen, I think my favorite fashion designer is my grandma Bucka. When I was little, she would design intricate clothes for my Corolle baby doll (I didn't want my baby to be a girl, so I named her Michael!). Well, thanks to Bucka, Michael had stunning ensembles: matching tops and bottoms with pretty buttons and fancy ribbons; chic matching hats. My baby was always the best dressed on the block.

Family has always been a huge influence on my fashion taste. My mom is an art teacher, so her love of color definitely rubbed off on me. In fact, in my yearbook, it says "Whitney Port: Most Likely to . . . invent her own highlighter color." But the rest of my style, that's all my own. I have never been one to conform. From the time I was old enough to dress myself, I liked to push the envelope in a tasteful, fun way. My fashion staples when I was a teen were lived-in Hard Tail sweats, UGG boots, checkered Vans, jean jackets, and anything rhinestoned. Then I got turned on to lingerie—but I couldn't keep it covered up! When I was thirteen, I was invited to bar and bat mitzvahs where most girls loved to step out in elegant evening dresses. What I wore to the parties were pieces of lingerie from Only Hearts. I wasn't channeling Madonna; I just had no chest, so the silky slips fit well and were comfy and looked ultrafeminine. I'd sometimes even pick up a lacy tank and silk pj bottoms and wear them as an outfit. I remember wearing a velvet snake-

Family has always been a huge influence on my fashion taste.

skin skirt and top with lace edging to my best friend's bat mitzvah. I can't believe my parents let me walk out the door like that! When girls wore fancy dresses to the high school semiformal, I wore a turquoise lace crop top with butterflies and rhinestones. Yes, you could say I liked to make an entrance.

Lover of fashion for as long as I can remember. (Mama has some good taste as well—she dressed us.)

My style has evolved based on my job and my location. When I was in high school, I was very carefree. But I didn't make fashion a huge priority. I'm a jeans and T-shirt girl. In high school, it was relaxed: Hard Tail or Juicy sweats and UGG boots were my uniform. In college at USC when I was in L.A., my look was a lot more California girl—I wore cowboy boots and little fun flirty dresses that were definitely more revealing. Then as I got into fashion, I started to follow designers and trends more. I never really cared about labels, but now I like to mix and match high and low end. Today, my go-to style is some sort of high-waisted, glitzy skirt with a tee tucked in, a blazer on top, and a pair of ankle boots. I pay more at-

I love mixing patterns and textures. Matching is too boring for me!

tention now to the complete look as opposed to just throwing separates together.

When filming *The City*, I rarely wear the same thing twice. As fun as that sounds, it's not easy, especially because I have no budget for clothes or even a stylist on set. It's all up to me, which is why I just recently hired my own stylist, Lara Backmender, to help me pull looks together when I'm crazy busy. And now that I'm a designer, I can wear my own line whenever I want, wherever I want. I love to show off my designs and represent the line.

So from Hard Tails to YSL, I have certainly redefined my fashion philosophy over the years. I realized that by putting just a little more effort into choosing an outfit and thinking outside the box, and outside of what's easiest, I can express myself in my clothes. Sometimes my outfits will earn raves, and other times they elicit some pretty puzzled looks, but I don't care either way. For me, fashion is about being inventive and creative; it's playing with color, cut, texture, and pattern, and mixing them up or blending them to achieve something fresh, new, and exciting. It's an art form. My fashion rule of thumb is simple: be who you are. If you were to ask me to explain my style, I'd have to say "contemporary funk mixed with classic femininity." Translation: it's hard to put a label on my look, and I like it that way.

Whitney, you say, this may work for you. But how can I march to my own fashion drummer and look polished and stylish? Here's the thing: you have to take a few risks. You can't be worried about what someone will think. That said, I wouldn't tell you to wear a bikini and sarong to a black-tie event (unless the theme was Hawaiian Luau!). But you could wear a sexy splash of floral print and liven up that stuffy room.

The idea is to interpret fashion so that it works for you. Think of it as putting your own special spin on an outfit—like I did with those formal-looks-gone-funky for my dances. I "Whitneyfy" my outfit each day to incorporate styles from all differ-

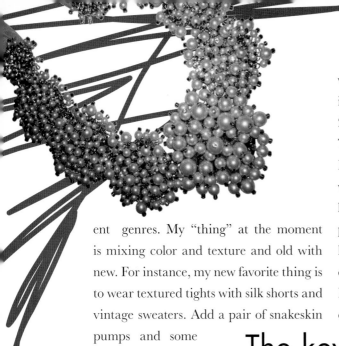

ent genres. My "thing" at the moment is mixing color and texture and old with new. For instance, my new favorite thing is to wear textured tights with silk shorts and vintage sweaters. Add a pair of snakeskin pumps and some bold costume jewelry and I'm all set!

Maybe this look isn't exactly your style; that's fine. You should never copy what someone is wearing just because they're wearing it. And what's trendy today may not be right for you. If it's not something you'd feel comfortable in—but you like *some* part of the look—then do it your way. And no one expects you to get it right every day; where would the world (and the celebrity weeklies!) be without fashion faux pas? I have had my share. I remember wearing a red minidress with black dots all over it, paired with a black braided belt with black stockings and ankle boots, to *The Hills* Season 2 premiere party at Area in Hollywood. The whole cast was there, and I thought I looked cute when I left the house. But when I saw myself in photos . . . yikes. I looked like a giant ladybug! I was a complete fashion nightmare. To top it off, I had these horrible Curly Sue ringlets all over my head. So Shirley Temple meets Ladybug. Hands down one of the worst outfits I've ever worn.

The key is to fill your wardrobe with clothes that work together effortlessly.

I am also not always a fountain of fashion ideas. Trust me; there are many mornings where I rip through my closet and want to wave a white flag in surrender. I can't find a thing to wear. Nada. Nothing fits, matches, or is clean/unwrinkled or remotely cute. Sound familiar? I keep a binder

Me at age seven, with my sister Paige, age five. Even at a young age I took fashion risks and wore highlighter-colored leopard-print outfits!

to build upon those basics. As you get more adept at fashion, you'll develop a "sixth sense" for what works together and what works for you. Picking out an outfit the night before also saves a lot of time and energy. In high school, I used to lay out my outfits on the floor from top to bottom, with accessories and all.

of torn-out fashion magazine spreads that I like, and sometimes I will try to emulate outfits from those shoots with my own clothes. The key is to fill your wardrobe with clothes that work together effortlessly (see the section "The Basics: Building Your Style" on p. 78), and you'll have less outfit agita. The way you achieve "style" is

WHO IS YOUR STYLE ICON?

When you're exploring your fashion personality, it helps to have a frame of reference. Who are the actors/personalities who embody your style philosophy? Are you an Elle Woods . . . or a Jackie O? Would you kill for Sarah Jessica Parker's style or do you prefer Posh Spice? The point is not to copy your style crush completely; instead, use her as a role model for what you're trying to achieve, be it sophistication and elegance (Audrey Hepburn, Cate Blanchett), boho chic (Kate Hudson, Keira Knightley, Ashley Olsen), or even rebel rocker (Rihanna, Kate Moss). Study what these women do with their ensembles: how they pair things together, accessorize, emphasize certain features. Then when you're putting together your own looks, channel your style icon's vibe. I have a huge list of icons, both old and new—but here are a few of my all-time faves:

Princess Diana

Shy Di (remember the high-necked frilly blouses?) transformed herself into the epitome of a powerful '90s woman. Her gowns were sleek and showed off her incredible legs and strong shoulders. She also embraced color (one of her favorites was bright red) and was the first in the royal family to be photographed both in jeans and a bikini! She took the stuffiness out of royal dressing and showed the world how to look and act like a modern girl!

Bianca Jagger

The woman was married to Mick, palled around with Warhol, and was Halston's muse. Need I say more? She truly embodied the image of fun-loving party girl back in the '70s disco age (who else would have the guts to ride a white horse into her thirtieth birthday bash at Studio 54?). I love that she has always taken fashion risks: her wedding gown had a deep, plunging neckline (so much for blushing bride!), and to this day she experiments with color, pattern, texture. She's even raided the men's department. Because she has such confidence in her style, she makes even the most over-the-top outfit the envy of everyone in the room.

Brigitte Bardot

The beautiful French actress was the essence of ooh-la-la sexy in the '60s; she's credited for making the bikini popular and for turning "bed head" into a hairstyle! She projected "sex kitten" no matter what she wore, although *j' adore* her pencil skirts and figure-hugging dresses with that French attention to flirty detail.

Faye Dunaway

What a fabulous femme fatale! As the gun-toting gangster moll in *Bonnie and Clyde*, she strutted confidently in slim tailored skirts, seductively tied silk scarves, and flirty berets (not to mention that chic bob!). She proved that you can be both feminine and strong. We should all take notes!

Mary-Kate and Ashley Olsen

Who would have thought those adorable twins on *Full House* would grow up to be two of the coolest fashion role models for our generation? MK and A are edgy; I'm not sure I would have the courage to wear what critics have dubbed their "bag lady chic." But these sisters flaunt their fearlessness. They launched two high-end fashion lines in 2008, Elizabeth and James, and the Row—and proved they have major designing chops as well as personal style. Brava times two!

Keira Knightley

I love the British aspect of her style, and how she mixes masculine and feminine. One day she does London street chic, and the next day she's superpolished at a premiere. She knows how to accentuate her figure and also how and when to take chances. Her style is always eclectic, but she *always* gets it right.

Rihanna

Coolness personified. She takes big fashion risks, mixing rocker with runway, but always with confidence. She puts out the vibe "I can be different and I'm okay with it." She doesn't just wear outfits, she rocks them!

THE BASICS: BUILDING YOUR STYLE

Every building needs a foundation, and the same goes for your style. The following are some basic pieces that can serve as building blocks for your wardrobe. The best part is, they all match with anything and everything—so you can create dozens of looks with just these ten easy pieces.

1 *Great-fitting jeans.*

I'm partial to Genetic Jeans and Current/Elliott at the moment and I went through a J Brand phase. But every girl has a brand that works best for her. I find that you'll get the most wear out of a darker wash; they're a little "dressier," so you can wear them to work as well as out at night. Do not feel like you have to spend a fortune for a fancy label. For how to find the perfect pair, see page 108. Another word of caution: although jeans with tears and holes are fine for weekends, you prob-ably won't be wearing this look to the office. Keep them for when you can be casual or funk them up for a night on the town.

2 *A little black dress (or LBD).*

This piece is a simple, flattering dress in the most universally slenderizing color (although any dark color, like navy or chocolate brown, is also fine). But that's just the beginning. Add a leather jacket over it, and you've got an edgy outfit for partying; sweep on a cashmere cardigan and it goes to work. Dress it up, dress it down; the LBD is the most versatile piece of clothing you can own. I like my hemlines short; just above the knee is most versatile. But it's really up to you, as is the neckline and the length of the sleeves. Just make sure the cut flatters your figure, and that the material is fairly good quality so it will last and last and last (you don't want it to come apart at the seams after just a few wears). Since this is a staple, you can also spend a bit more for a good dress; you'll get a lot of wear out of it. But that said, you will often find a great LBD on the sale rack. If the price is right, snatch up a few in different cuts and weights. You won't regret it.

3

Simple white, black, or heather gray tanks/tees.

They work under anything—a suit jacket, a sheer blouse, a low-cut sweater—or tucked into a cute skirt. They should be soft, supple, and comfy. And when it's hot in the summer, you can wear them solo! If you find a bargain price, buy a bunch.

4

A leather jacket.

A motorcycle jacket is a cool classic; for elegance, you can't beat a luxe leather trench (my fave is by DVF!). Leather is expensive, but it's a long-term investment. The right leather jacket can go with everything from jeans to a sundress and last for years. Black is the most versatile color, though if you're bold, you can also get a lot of wear out of red, brown, a metallic hue, light

gray, navy, or worn-out leather. Sometimes if I have a jacket that looks "too new," I'll put it on the floor and stomp on it!

5

Cashmere knit scarves in any color.

If my outfit needs a little "oomph," a bright scarf saves the day. Drape one around your neck; tuck it under the collar of a coat; sweep it around your shoulders as a shawl for evening; even tie it on your bag handle to add color. Wait till they go on sale after New Year's, then stock up on several shades. I have a nude one that I wear almost every day that matches everything. My mom always says if your neck is warm, you're set! Great as travel blankets as well.

6 Black boots.

I love them in all lengths: short, medium, tall, over the knee. You can really wear them with anything, from skinny jeans to a long, flowing skirt. But not all boots are created equal. The other day, Kelly cleaned out her closet and brought a bag of them to work. Roxy wanted this mid-calf-length studded pair with a squared-off toe. Hideous! I put the kibosh on it—and I know why Kel was trying to get rid of them!

7 A black (or navy) blazer.

Classic and classy. I toss one on with trousers, a floaty sundress, even a tee and jeans. I feel like it adds instant polish and "seriousness" to my outfit. Right now, I am into the oversize men's suit jacket look. It makes a simple outfit a little edgier.

8 Simple heels (2–3 inches).

Again, black is an easy choice since it goes with anything, but I am a huge fan of colorful shoes. Bright jewel tones jazz up a plain suit or a neutral-colored dress. The style, again, is up to you: pumps, mules, slingbacks, wedges, clogs, ankle straps . . . whatever you feel you'll get the most use out of for work/play. I stay away from anything too pointy—it reminds me of a witch.

9 A sleek pencil skirt.

The most versatile hemline hits just at the knee or slightly above/below, but show as much leg as you like. You can wear this day or night, paired with anything from a businessy blouse to a sexy tank. Pencil skirts are an ideal cut—sophisticated and versatile for day or night.

10 *An accessory that adds polish.*

My personal pick would be gold or silver hoop earrings, since they literally work with anything. But here's where your personality comes into play. You could choose a simple pair of studs (Claire's has tons that are cheap!), a dramatic pendant, layered long chains, a belt, a jeweled hair piece, or a stack of bangles. The goal is to find one "wow" addition that will work with a multitude of outfits. I often wear gold and silver chains wrapped around my wrist—another great use for a simple necklace.

WHAT I'M LOVING IN MY WARDROBE RIGHT NOW

Kate Spade cashmere sweaters

Isabel Marant jacket

Rachel Comey dresses and shorts

Whyred textured leggings from Opening
  Ceremony in black, navy, and maroon

Bandeaux bras

Fluffy soft socks, great for travel

DVF leather trench coat

DVF sequin jacket

Whitney Eve velvet dresses and slacks

Chanel nude purse

Topshop studded flats

Kain T-shirts

Marc Jacobs buckle boots

Lulu Frost, Fenton Fallon, Bing Bang,
  Made Her Think, and CC Skye jewelry

Giuseppe Zanotti shoes

Miu Miu shoes and bags

Converse leather high tops

Dr. Martens work boots

Chloe over-the-knee boots

  Loeffler Randall boots (get the point?
    I love BOOTS!)

    Victoria's Secret
      bathing suits

        Valentino heels

Topshop heels and bags . . .
  Topshop anything!

Gucci tapestry bag

Bloch flats; Sue London flats

Alexander Wang tees

Wolford tights

Current Elliot cords

Tacori stud earrings

White & Warren scarves and sweaters

Moschino jackets and shoes

Genetic jeans

Vena Cava jumper

Jen Kao dresses and skirts

Rebecca Taylor skirts and dresses

Be & D bags

Chanel chain messenger bag

Rebecca Minkoff
  studded bags

And duh! My own line,
  Whitney Eve! Especially
  my oversize blazer

TRY IT . . . YOU MIGHT LIKE IT

Occasionally, you'll be surprised when you try something new on—something totally out of your fashion realm—and it looks *amazing*. I am lucky to have a truly gifted stylist, Lara Backmender, who pulls looks for events and the red carpet. She can spot an outfit on the rack or on the runway and know instinctively I'll flip over it. But every now and then, she'll throw me a curveball. She'll show me something and I'll think, "No, no, no . . . so *not* me." Then I remember, "Well, the woman is a professional . . . she is one of the best in the business!" And I almost always love it. What I'm saying here is this: have an open mind when it comes to fashion. If your best friend, boyfriend, sis, or even the salesperson suggests you try something on, don't automatically say no because it's something you wouldn't normally wear. It's hard to tell how something will look on you when it's on the hanger. But don't be peer pressured into wearing anything—the most important thing is that you feel comfortable in it.

One of my pet peeves is when salespeople try to push things on me.

Sometimes you'll be shocked by what you end up being drawn to. Just ask my little

The most important thing is that you feel comfortable in it.

sister, Paige, who recently "borrowed" a pair of boots from me that, in the past, she would not have been caught dead in. Paige went to school in the middle of Wisconsin and didn't need to be a fashionista. She looks at some of the things I wear in utter shock or horror. But then she moved back to L.A. and decided maybe it was time for a change. She called to inform me that she had found these crazy leopard platform ankle boots that I had left at home: "Whit, I tried them on and I am totally wearing them out this weekend!" I had to laugh just picturing my no-frills sis strutting out in those boots—but I'm so glad she's taking fashion risks and having fun!

SHOULD YOU BUY "HIGH"?

A lot of people are very label conscious. They think that paying a fortune for something designer equals status. Not me. I am a big believer in mixing high end and low end. I have no problem pairing an inexpensive T-shirt and jeans with designer heels. I love poking around through vintage stores and flea markets and scooping up steals. But I totally get it; sometimes, that pricey Chloe bag is just begging you, "Buy me!"

When you're just starting out, you probably don't have a lot of money to spend on high end. That's okay. Think about what you really want/need and what will be a good investment piece. For me, it's often a great bag. I carry one every day, so it's going to get plenty of airing. But it also has to be strong enough to tote all my stuff to and from work and survive getting knocked around on the NYC subways and streets. One of the first expensive bags I bought when I came here was a black Chanel backpack. I liked that I could have my hands free when I wore it, and also that I could wipe it clean if

it got spilled on, dropped, trampled, and so on. So although it cost a lot more than the backpacks I used to carry in college, I have definitely gotten my money's worth out of it. I wear it every day—although my friends tease me that I've never outgrown my backpack days. Bags also *never* go out of style, unless it's one of those teddy bear backpacks my sisters and I wore in elementary school.

If you fall in love with an item that's not in your price range, don't give up so easily. Comparison shop at several stores. Ask the salesperson when it might be reduced— or if there are any coupons that will slice a percentage off the price tag. Google it and see if any of the discount fashion sites like bluefly.com, net-a-porter.com, ruelala. com, gilt.com, or shopbop.com carry it or a similar style. Even the department store Web sites have awesome sales. Often, you can find a bag you love in a "less popular" color—like green, pink, or purple. If you're like me and you love color, this is a good thing! Or sometimes "off-season" bags will be reduced, so you can get a great white

Gucci tote in the middle of the winter for a steal.

With a little ingenuity, you can find luxury for less. One of my friends was lusting over a sexy red suede Prada purse. On her editorial assistant salary, she just couldn't justify spending a week's salary when she had to eat and pay rent. Then she saw it one day for 40 percent off on bluefly! Score! Just make sure if you're buying designer off the Web, you're getting it from a trusted online merchant, like any of the ones mentioned. I had another, less-savvy friend who bought a **YSL Muse** bag off eBay, only to discover—after she paid $500 for it—that it was a fake.

You can also find a lot of clothing that has that couture "feel" without the hefty price tag. I love stores like H&M, Forever 21, Target, Urban Outfitters, Topshop.com, and pixiemarket.com. You can find everything from work clothes to evening wear for under $100! Another secret to looking like you spent $500 when you've really spent $50? Tailoring. A good tailor will be able to nip and tuck so that your clothes skim your body like they were custom-made. It generally will cost you an additional $20–$40 or so per item, but it's worth every penny if your outfit fits you like a glove.

SHOULD IT STAY OR SHOULD IT GO?

If you're going to buy new things, you have to purge your closets and drawers of items that no longer work for you. It kills me to get rid of my clothes. Seriously, I get totally sentimental over dresses I have worn to special occasions (even high school dances). I am emotionally attached! Sometimes I fear I'm becoming a hoarder! That said, I needed more space in my first place, and my wardrobe was taking up 99 percent of it. So I edited my closet—painful as it was. Buh-bye raggedy sweatshirts and sweats and bras that don't fit! Adios to ten of the same white tees and tanks! Get your best friend (someone who will be 100 percent honest with you) by your side for a give-away session. Should it stay or should it go?

Also, if you have sisters or female cousins, keep it in the family. That way you can always take it back if you regret giving it away.

Always swapping clothes with my sisters. In fact, that was the only thing we would ever bicker about.

Three simple rules will help you decide.

1 Don't hold on to ancient clothes thinking you'll lose weight. One pair of skinny jeans in the back of the closet is incentive enough.

2 When in doubt, try it on. If it doesn't fit, has frays, tears, or stains . . . it's outta there! Donate, donate, donate!

3 If you haven't worn something in the last year (or since high school!), you will probably *never* wear it again. Clear it out to make room for new stuff.

My closet before I got organized. I gave my sisters the pieces that just didn't inspire me anymore.

MY FAVE FASHION HITS AND MISSES

Sometimes you get it right . . . and sometimes you get it wrong. Really wrong. As in someone call the fashion police wrong. And you don't even realize it until you see a photo of yourself. Even someone who follows fashion (that would be me!) has the occasional "What was I thinking?" moment. Truth be told, we all have those days when our outfit is a little off or out of character—mine just tend to show up on TV or in the dos and don'ts pages of magazines.

Here are five of my chicest red carpet moments and four of my all-time worst fashion faux pas. All you can do is laugh at the bad ones (can you say "Ladybug dress"?) and learn from them. You can give away the don'ts to Goodwill or keep them as hand-me-downs—everything comes back into style eventually. I also find they sometimes make good Halloween costumes . . .

The Hits

I love these looks for lots of different reasons:

It always looks so fresh and effortless to pair your favorite jeans with a tank and feminine blazer. Wear them with a funky heel and there is really not much you have to do to look chic and cute without trying too hard. It's one of those outfits that you can throw on when nothing in your closet is working.

I wore this in Las Vegas on a trip when my suitcase got lost. I scoured the Caesars Palace Forum Shops and finally found this Marc Jacobs dress. It was so comfortable and had such a flattering cut. I'm a sucker for turtlenecks and anything short!

I was honored to be invited to the Council of Fashion Designers of America Awards representing Luca Luca in their gorgeous gown. The way the back crisscrossed was so sexy, and I just felt incredibly elegant. I loved the steel blue color as well.

This was a vintage beaded dress that my stylist, Lara, found. It had such gorgeous hand beading and the pastel color was so creamy and pretty. I faked a bob to show off the sheer top of the dress.

92 Whitney Port

Another effortless look to try: tuck a
white tank into a comfy, textured, high-
waisted black skirt and you've got the
cocktail/going-out-dancing look down!
Those T-strap heels with the little black
poof are still one of my favorites! I wore
them to my first interview at DVF and
got so many compliments.

The Misses

Lucky me: if my parents didn't snap some of my worst outfits over the years, then the paparazzi sure did!

I actually loved the print on this dress, but the colors didn't quite suit me and the cut covered too much on top. It also doesn't look great in photographs!

This is another one of my favorite dresses, in theory, but I think the cutout in the middle was too ahead of its time.

The main problem with this look is that it's all around just too big. The hat is not a red carpet kind of accessory, the jacket is not a cute fit on me, and the jeans are way too big and long. I don't think I was planning on going out when I put this outfit on!

My Ladybug look! Never dress like an insect unless it's Halloween. I have since banned ringlets from my hair "dos."

WHITTYISM: INSTANT SEX APPEAL!

Having a drab day? Put these on and you'll feel smokin' hot:

Lace panties.

No matter how hot your outfit is, there is no way in the world you're going to feel good about yourself if you're wearing "blah" undies. Splurge on a few fabulous pairs of lace ones. My faves are from Hanky Panky (hankypanky.com). They're so soft and comfy; they never ride up.

A sexy bra.

Cleavage can give you such a boost (pun intended), and if you don't have ample of your own, a great bra can work wonders. I'm personally bonkers over Bellabumbum bras, probably because they come in all these great, bright colors like peacock green and lilac (my fave). They're supercomfy; they never pinch, and you can literally lounge around your place in them. Just don't let the neighbors get an eyeful . . .

Stilettos.

Slip 'em on and you instantly feel sexy, skinny, and tall. Of course, if you're going to cram your feet into mile-high shoes, you better be prepared:

- Go shoe shopping in the afternoon when your feet are most swollen to get a real idea of what the heels will feel like after you've been in them for hours. Also, have the salesperson measure your foot—the way you used to when you were a kid—so you know the size is correct.
- If the shoe is really high and really pointy, try a half size to a full size larger than you'd normally wear. This will prevent pinching. And toe cleavage is not attractive!
- Buy some foot pads or insoles (I like the squishy gel ones)—they'll help prevent pain and blistering. I wore the ones by Dr. Scholl's to my sis's wedding and they saved the day!

- Break your heels in. You shouldn't buy a new pair and wear them out five minutes later for a night of dancing or a day at the office. Walk around the block in them or, at the very least, wear them around your home for a few hours, allowing the shoe to mold to the shape of your foot. Also, scuff the soles so you don't slip. You can also take a key and "engrave" some marks in the soles to make them less slippery.

ASK WHITNEY: WHAT SHOULD I WEAR WHEN . . .

"I am meeting my boyfriend's parents for the first time . . ."

Think class, not sass. A dress is always an appropriate option as long as it's not too form-fitting, short, or low-cut. You want your man to say, "Dad, Mom . . . this is my girlfriend." Not, "Dad, Mom, this is my girlfriend and her boobs!" Bend over and make sure you're covered both on top and bottom. Try not to wear too much makeup (they'll think their son is dating one of the girls from _Jersey Shore_!). Keep it natural. It's also a good idea to coordinate with your guy. If he's in a suit, don't wear jeans and a sweater. Follow his lead; he knows his folks best. And finally—here's my no-fail "impress the parents" tip: add a touch of heirloom jewelry to your look, maybe a broach or a bracelet from your mom or grandmother. It will definitely be a conversation starter, and it shows you care about family (brownie points!).

"I have a blind date . . ."

It all depends on what you are doing and where you're going. In general, you want to avoid anything too revealing or over the top. Better to get to know him a little first before you bare your soul or any other private parts. For casual dates—like a movie—I would go for a skinny pant or jean, maybe a cute comfy sweater, and boots or flats. For something a little more formal—like dinner at a nice restaurant—you can't go wrong with a nice pencil skirt, sophisticated blouse, bomber jacket, and some comfortable heels. Most important, wear something that's "you," that makes you feel confident and at ease. I recently went on a dinner date and wore a deep purple velvet, long-sleeved V-neck Jill Stuart minidress with La Perla black tights and snakeskin heels. I added dangly chandelier earrings and wore deep red lipstick and did my hair retro chic wavy for drama. I felt alluring . . . but not overexposed.

"I am meeting my ex for drinks . . ."

Hot-hot-hot is the only way to go! Show him what he is missing! I met up with my ex Jay for drinks a few weeks after we broke up and I wanted to show him how together I was after we split. So I wore a slinky heather gray Jen Kao minidress—it had long sleeves but was skintight—with high heels and a little clutch, and I wore my hair down stick straight! You want your look to say, "You know you want me . . . and you blew it, dude."

"To the company holiday party . . ."

Remember who you're partying with: the people you work with. You don't want to be the water cooler conversation Monday morning. You should loosen up a little from your day look and dress festive—but keep cleavage in check. I'd suggest a V-neck sheath dress, a bright colored blouse and skirt, or a wide-leg pant with an embellished top. Dazzling accessories are totally acceptable: a great oversize or embellished clutch or chunky jewelry accents with fun hues.

"On a weekend getaway when I don't want to look like a slob . . ."

A few changes are all you really need. Stick to fabulous, versatile pieces that you can mix and match. My must-have for a short getaway is a maxidress. It works for most body types, packs easily, and can be worn with any type of sandals or flats for day and heels for evening. I take one in a soft, pretty pattern. I also never travel without a big, neutral-colored scarf. It can be used as a blanket while en route, a wrap to the beach or pool, or anytime you need a little extra warmth. Pack a comfy pair of shoes as well—a cute pair of comfy ballerina flats or a pair of Converse, Keds, or Vans work. And you can't go wrong with a comfy, baggy pair of jeans; a simple skirt with an elastic waist or a little ruffling; and a few cute tops.

"On a plane . . ."

Since it can get steamy standing in a crowded airport check-in line, and chilly on an air-conditioned plane, I always dress in layers that can be peeled off or added as needed. A sweater, hoodie, or thick scarf over a simple tank or tee will look stylish and also be practical. If only I always followed my own advice! I was recently on a red-eye from L.A., figuring I'd never see anyone I knew, and I wore sweats, UGGs, and an oversize long, hooded sweater. I looked a mess—and of course I bumped into two guys on the plane who were friends with the guy I'm dating. I only hope they weren't snapping pics and e-mailing them to him! Also, stick to comfy slip-on shoes—like ballet slippers or loafers. You'll be asked to take them off when going through security, and you might have to walk miles to the gate. Definitely not fun in heels! Don't forget to pack a pair of thick, fluffy socks in your carry-on—feet get so cold on planes.

On my way to Australia, all bundled up in my cashmere wrap.

My first view of Australia from the plane window.

Paige and I were folding clothes for a one-week trip. I always overpack; I like to be superprepared when I'm away. I also like to separate by categories: dresses, skirts, sweaters, shorts, etc., so when I unpack it's that much easier!

short numbers as well. Glamour isn't what it used to be. I love a dress that's simple and backless . . . I think it's so subtly sexy. You look good coming and going! The style and the glitz factor is up to you. Just make sure it flatters your figure and you can move in it. A friend of mine bought a gorgeous fish-tail gown for a formal benefit . . . only to discover she couldn't step up the stairs to the venue because it was so tight!

"The invitation says 'black tie' . . ."

Black tie means *very* formal. It doesn't mean you actually have to wear black; I certainly wear bold colors for evening affairs. But it does mean guests will be dressed to the nines, men in tuxes and women in long gowns of silk, satin, or sequins. You can be a little "looser" when you're younger—you can go shorter or show a little more skin. I brought my best friend, Andrea, to a black-tie event and we ended up agreeing that her short, beaded, one-shoulder silk dress was appropriate. Surprisingly, many other women were in

COLOR ME STYLISH!

Dearie, why so drab? If there is one fashion lesson you learn from me, let it be this: a little color is good for the soul! I believe in injecting a bit of brightness into every outfit. It brings out the highlights in your hair, warms your complexion, even adds sparkle to your eyes. Color makes you feel alive, energized, confident.

I believe in injecting a bit of brightness into every outfit.

Whether you add just a hint (a bright chunky chain necklace to a black dress) or pile it on (a bright scarf, boots, and bag with a tan trench), there are so many ways to weave it into your wardrobe. Don't be afraid to mix and match complementing colors. Some color combos I like are navy and light pink, lavender and nude, coral and turquoise. Certain hair colors/complexions look better in specific colors. It's hard to judge what your best palette is until you've tried on several colors. My best colors are definitely nude, lavender, coral, and aqua, while no can do yellow and orange.

Roxy, even though she claims to be the only California girl who wears black all the time, actually wore a Kelly green dress on a double date with me in the Meatpacking District—I think I'm beginning to rub off on her—and she absolutely glowed in the color. And my girlfriend Sammy rocked HOT bubblegum pink heels with a simple black dress to an art gallery opening. I love it! Both my girls admit that when you wear a little color, not only do you feel good . . . but you get a guy's attention. As Martha Stewart would say, "It's a good thing!"

Brunettes

Women with dark hair and dark eyes (including African Americans/Asians) look beautiful in bold, dramatic hues, like royal blue, crimson red, shocking pink, and emerald green.

Blondes

Women with lighter hair (or brunettes with light eyes) glow in springy shades, like lavender, mauve, nude, seafoam, and coral.

Redheads

Redheads look radiant in colors with golden undertones, like camel, beige, orange, gold, and chocolate.

Can you tell I love color and crazy patterns? Lime green, hot pink, bright yellow—bring it on!

BREAKING THE RULES

Never wear white after Labor Day. Don't combine gold and silver jewelry. Different patterns should never mix. It's time to ditch these tired rules! I see nothing wrong with wearing white year-round or donning glitter, shine, and embellishments during the day to spice up your daily grind. I think it's cool and fun to prove the rules wrong. I once wore a horizontal white-and-navy-striped Alexander Wang sweater with a Wayne plaid jacket. Not a natural combo, I know, but I thought it looked really funky together.

Just because you're not a size 0 and you have some curves doesn't mean you can't wear form-fitting clothes (can someone say J.Lo?). If you got it, flaunt it! And who ever said that you can't wear black with brown or navy was seriously mistaken. A black skirt and chocolate brown heels are a stunning mixture. And forget that old adage about your shoes having to match your bag. I recently spotted a woman on the street rocking a yellow oversize clutch with red pumps—what a look!

So what rules—if any—should you follow? This is the only one I subscribe to: don't wear something *just* because it's trendy. If you like it, fine. But if the only reason you're putting it on is because it's on some magazine's "In" list, I want you to think twice. It's like my mom used to say, "If someone told you to jump off a bridge with them, would you?" You need to develop your fashion backbone; resist the urge to splurge on stuff that isn't "you." Case in point: a few years ago, fedoras made a huge comeback. You know, the Dick Tracy–like detective hats? I passed. I don't care how many stars in Hollywood were wearing them. On me, they looked ridiculous.

I also believe you should never be *too* revealing with your outfits. Sexy is one thing; skanky is another. Adhere to the rules of common decency. Do not be caught with your pants down (or off!) in public or step out of a cab and flash the world your ass-ets. If your dress is low-cut, make sure there is something (such as double-sided Hollywood Fashion Tape) keeping your boobs under wraps. I know, sometimes it's an accident. But here's my golden rule: you can avoid major wardrobe malfunctions by simply checking every angle in the mirror as you sit, squat, bend, and jump. And don't forget to check yourself out in bright or natural light; how many times have I seen some poor girl strut into a party only to discover her dress or blouse was completely see-through? If you've done my check, you're good to go, lady.

JEAN-EOLOGY: FIND THE PERFECT PAIR

Studies say that women spend more time shopping for jeans than any other item of clothing, an average of three hours each shopping trip! But all that work can be worth it—jeans are easily the most versatile piece in your wardrobe. But with so many cuts, washes, and styles to choose from—not to mention an endless array of brands and price ranges—it truly is a mission to find one pair of denim that does it all. No matter what you think will look best on you—or even what has in the past—you have to try jeans on to really make certain. Choose a store that will let you take your time; go through fifty pairs if you feel like it. If they're snooty or trying to rush you to make a decision (or give up the dressing room), go somewhere else. I like to shop for jeans at department stores and Urban Outfitters. Skinny jeans are my fave

because they elongate the legs, and I prefer them soft with some give, not stiff. An added bonus: if I can score a pair that also boosts my butt. My biggest thing with jeans is they have to be comfortable. I hate when they're too tight around my waist. My go-to style is low-waist, stretch, dark skinny jeans.

Your jeans should fit you *now;* not when you lose five pounds, not when you "break them in." Denim will stretch . . . but not that much. Figure 10 percent. If they're really tight in the waist or thighs, chances are they're not going to loosen up enough to really be comfy. So make sure can you sit, squat, and bend in them without cutting off circulation. And make sure your undies don't stick out when you bend over; that's just tacky.

Once you get your jeans home, always wash them in cold water. Warm water will shrink them. Turn them inside out to prevent fading, and skip the fabric softener (it can also break up the dye). Air-dry them instead of tossing them in the dryer, and dry-clean your dressier ones so they stay dark and crisp looking. Dirty side note: I may wear jeans five times or more before washing them. It's okay!

IT'S NOT WHAT YOU WEAR, BUT HOW YOU WEAR IT

Corny as it sounds, confidence is your best accessory. It doesn't matter how expensive or adorable that outfit is; if you feel awful about yourself, you'll look awful in it. I can look at a picture of myself and tell you if I was having a good day or a bad day by whether I have that frazzled look on my face. Which is a pity, because sometimes I really loved the outfit I was wearing and I let my bad attitude spoil the perfect photo op.

We all feel insecure about ourselves sometimes (I don't even want to tell you how nervous I was when they filmed me in a bikini on *The City*!). You think you'll grow out of it when you graduate from college. Adults don't doubt themselves, do they? Of course we do. We all have something we don't like about our bodies; some days, I am horrified by my love handles (now you understand the bikini anxiety). But no one is perfect. If you were, you'd be made out of plastic . . . or married to Seal. What I'm saying is, don't hate Heidi Klum because she's beautiful, and don't hate yourself because some days you feel anything but. Focus on your most fabulous features—your beautiful smile, your shiny hair, your sparkling eyes—not every flaw you can find in the mirror (and only if you look really, really hard). If you can't give yourself an attitude adjustment, call a friend or a family member for a pep talk before you set foot out that door. Stand up tall, hold your head high, take a deep breath, smile, and tell yourself, "I look *gooood*," and mean it. Suddenly, you'll radiate confidence and charisma; people will be drawn to you like a magnet and ask you what diet you're on or if you've cut your hair. Maybe they won't be able to put their finger on what it is that's different, but you'll know . . . you're "wearing" your confidence!

CHAPTER FOUR

PARTIES

No more keggers and Domino's pizza like in college. When you're in your twenties, soirees are about celebrating friendships, relaxing, and blowing off a little steam. I go to parties—mostly premieres or fashion events—at least twice a week. They're often glamorous and I get dressed up, but having people over in your personal space makes the event much more of a reflection of you. I always loved the idea of throwing a party in *my very own apartment*. It is a chance to showcase my lovely space, my unique taste, and celebrate the fact that (*Yes!*) I was not only surviving, but thriving in NYC! So with some help from my very talented party planner sister, Ashley, I have become quite the hostess over the last few years.

I was really excited about "entertaining"—it had such an elegant "adult" ring to it. I had been to an over-the-top dinner party on Olivia's posh Tribeca rooftop—that was quite the get-together. But I knew that *my* party would be different. It would be filled with cool people and great food, drinks, and music—and it would be intimate and relaxed, just like my apartment.

Roxy was my partner in crime—and truth be told, she talked me into it. I was living in my new apartment in the West

Ashley's wedding day: (left to right) Jade, Paige, Ryan, Ashley, Mom, Dad, and me!

Village—and she was staying with me at the time until she found her own place—so we decided to throw a housewarming party. I told Rox while we were planning it all out that we had to keep it low-key; the Board of my building didn't like music after eleven . . . but apparently that went in one ear and out the other. We agreed on a little cocktail party for a few friends. Instead, it was bigger than a block party—and the police wound up banging on our door! I was stuck at work at People's Revolution a little late that night, so Roxy had headed home to set up and greet our guests. By the time I got there, I saw the floods of people in my living room downing shots and drinking Roxy's signature superstrong jungle juice.

I'm not quite sure how it got so out of control (or who all those people were!). I freaked and just kept thinking, *Please, don't let me get kicked out of my new apartment!* Then came the sirens . . . Well, I did realize one thing: the next time I decided to throw a

Family portrait: (clockwise from back left) Ryan, Mom, Dad, Me, Ashley, Jade, Paige.

party in my place, I would (a) ask my sister Ashley for advice and (b) rein in Rox. That said, it wasn't all bad . . . just a bit chaotic.

So what makes a good party? Some people probably think an appearance by NYC's finest constitutes a pretty memorable bash (not me!). For others, it's all in the details. I have friends who go to great lengths folding little swan-shaped napkins and preparing exotic appetizers I can't pronounce, much less recognize. For other folks, it's about the ambiance: the right lighting, music, decorations. All of that helps, but if you ask me, the people are the most important component. If you have the people you love, your party will rock. There'll be intoxicating conversation, lots of laughs, even a few phone numbers exchanged. Pack a room with party poopers and your fete will fall flat. I always make

Singing karaoke with Roxy at my twenty-fifth birthday party in NYC.

sure I have a few chatty, colorful characters and some old reliable friends. You don't want everyone to necessarily know one another, but you do want people to feel comfortable. So make sure everyone you invite has at least has one "buddy" or acquaintance to schmooze with.

WHITNEY 101: HOW TO THROW A GREAT PARTY

Start with a fabulous idea.

By this, I mean figure out what the "theme" is. Are you throwing a Super Bowl Beer and Wings bash? An elegant sit-down dinner? A tea party for just the girls? Once you know the concept, you can plan the decorations, the guest list, and your menu—even if you only intend to order in.

Pick the perfect time.

A good party requires a good turnout. You may not want a huge party, but you still want people to come. Obviously, Friday or Saturday nights are the most popular times; you don't have to go to work the next morning. But sometimes a Sunday brunch can be just as fun! Just double-check that your party doesn't conflict with other popular events—like the World Series, Super Bowl, and so on—unless you are counting on that as part of your theme.

Invite your guests.

I know e-vites are all the rage because they're so easy (and free!), but I still think handwritten invitations are the way to go. They're so much more personal. Obviously if your party is last minute, you can call or e-mail. But it's a lot of fun to get creative. Your invite should obviously echo your theme. A friend of mine in New York threw a "Lobster Fest" on her rooftop and printed the who, what, where, and when in colored Sharpies on white disposable bibs. Very clever (and inexpensive!). When I was a kid, my mom always made our invitations by hand. It's so easy to hit a craft or paper store (like Michael's, Kate's Paperie, Staples) and score beautiful cardstock or paper you can print on or adorn by hand. Personalize your invite with stickers, scrapbooking cutouts, ribbons, glitter glue, photos, lace . . . whatever strikes your fancy. You can also find great templates online at sites like americangreetings.com. Make sure to include the essentials: date, place, time, theme (if any), BYOB, dating details (can you bring a plus one?) and include how to RSVP—via phone or e-mail. Maybe even come up with a cute poem for the invite. Ashley's husband is a songwriter and always comes up with the most witty invitation texts.

Decide what drinks and food to serve.

Make sure you have plenty for the number of people coming. I prefer to put things out buffet style and let people help themselves—it lets me mix and mingle and not worry about waiting on everyone. You should have enough chips, dips, nuts, and pretzels to keep people snacking all night. I would also suggest vegetable plates or different types of bruschetta for the more health conscious—I love to put out bowls of hummus and guacamole with crudités or cheese plates.

Size matters.

The number of people invited should be only ten greater than the space can hold (you hear that, Roxy?). Otherwise, you'll be packed in like a bunch of sardines. Not fun. A good rule of thumb: about 10 percent of your invitees will not attend. If you are inviting guests from out of town, the percentage is higher. If there are still people you've left off, create a "B" list. Just make sure your RSVP date leaves enough time till the party to invite your backups (at least a week is reasonable).

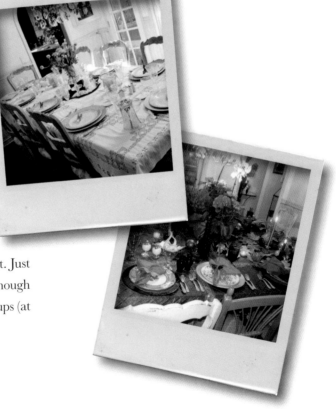

Set your sound track.

I like to put together a playlist of great tunes on my iPod—it can help to fill those awkward silences when the party is just starting. Some of my faves: Adele, the Kooks, the XX, La Roux, and Ratatat, and I love Dean Martin, Frank Sinatra, Etta James, John Legend, Tamarama, and Billie Holiday.

Drink up.

Unless you have a fully stocked bar and don't mind the expense, I would recommend having one type of drink to keep your costs lower—a signature cocktail, so to speak. Sangria is a great option, and you don't need to use a pricey bottle of cabernet. A simple red table wine for about $5 will do!

Make sure the space is set.

Do you have enough seats? Tables for people to put down plates/drinks? If not, borrow or rent. Make sure your guests have everything they'll need: enough napkins, plates, cups, and silverware—even TP in the bathroom! A good hostess covers all the bases. Don't forget the flowers!

HOW TO THROW A SMASHING . . .

Cocktail Party

Unless you have a lot of seating room (i.e., a dining table that has a leaf that folds out), a mix-and-mingle party—where you serve finger foods and cocktails—is the easiest to plan. Here's where you can get creative and devise a theme, like Mexican, Italian, Japanese. I love color themes, like a black-and-white theme à la Truman Capote, or even a metallic theme and playful themes, like "kid at heart" where you serve chicken nuggets, miniburgers, dogs, pizzas, and Popsicles! At one house party recently, the hostess devised her menu in her favorite colors, red and white. She put out tiny individual cups of pasta with a mushroom red sauce and platters of cherry tomatoes and mozzarella, and had pitchers of strawberry margaritas and white cosmos (made with white cranberry juice). Very cute! I also went to a really fun dessert party: little cupcakes, tarts, and cookies.

Be sure to scatter tons of napkins near the dishes—so people aren't dropping sauce or crumbs or wiping their fingers all over your furniture. If you have light-colored couches or chairs, buy inexpensive slipcovers or throws to protect them. They won't be as pretty, but you'll prevent stains, which are bound to happen with a big crowd!

Set the mood.

Dim the lights, fill the room with candles, and crank up some soft, subdued tunes (anything louder will be hard to talk over).

Serve up the apps.

I make sure to put out plates of different appetizers all around the room, so everyone can make their way around, chatting as they nibble and nosh. Cheese plates with grapes, Marcona almonds, and crackers and crudités with dip are a given, as are bowls of homemade bridge mix, pretzels, and chips. Beyond that, think savory snacks that are easy to pick up and pop in your mouth.

Mom's Chili Cheese Bites

Makes 32 "Bites"

This is an easy hors d'oeuvre that takes ten minutes max to get in the oven (a big plus when you're rushing to get dressed). When we entertained at home, my mom would have to double the ingredients and whip up a larger 9 x 13 pan because I would gobble up at least half of it before guests would arrive!

My mama.

4 tablespoons butter/margarine
5 eggs
¼ cup all-purpose flour
½ teaspoon baking powder
Dash of salt
1 (4 oz.) can chopped green chilies
½ pint small curd cottage cheese (1 cup)
2 cups shredded Monterey jack cheese

Preheat oven to 400 degrees Fahrenheit (205°C). Melt butter/margarine in a 9-inch-square pan in the oven (tip pan to coat bottom and sides). In a large bowl, beat the eggs, then stir in the flour, baking powder, and salt. Add the melted butter/margarine to the preceding; set pan aside. Stir in the chilies, cottage cheese, and jack cheese; mix until blended. Pour batter into the butter/margarine-coated pan. Bake 15 minutes. Reduce heat to 350 degrees and bake 30–35 minutes longer or until lightly browned. Cool slightly and cut into small squares. May be frozen. If frozen, before serving reheat in a 400-degree Fahrenheit oven for 10 minutes or until hot.

Easy Hummus Recipe

Makes 1 Cup

A Whitney staple. Hummus is one of my fave foods, and it's even better when you make it from scratch (you can really taste that garlic!). Feel free to go crazy and serve it with any kind of vegetables, pita, or chips.

½ cup chopped parsley
1 big garlic cloves minced
½ teaspoon salt
*3 tablespoons tahini sesame seed paste (can be purchased at most
    grocery stores or a gourmet shop)*
4 tablespoons lemon juice
1 (15½ oz.) can garbanzo beans, drained

Place all ingredients in a blender or food processor fitted with a metal blade. Process until smooth. Refrigerate several hours before serving, may be stored in fridge up to one month. Serve cold as a dip or spread.

Sangria in a Snap

2 bottles of red wine, standard size
2 oranges, cut into bite-size pieces with the skin on
2 apples, cut into bite-size pieces with the skin on
1 handful of any type of berries
12 oz. of 7-Up
1 half bottle Prosecco

This can be made ahead of time and stored in the refrigerator. Add the 7-Up and Prosecco at the end, right before you serve, to make sure the fizz holds. Make sure to tell guests to eat the fruit, too—it's the best part of sangria!

Toaster Oven Apps Party

My family will tell you that I am not exactly an Iron Chef in the kitchen. My mom, my sister Ashley, and my sis Paige—they can make a feast out of anything in the fridge. I am not as talented in the kitchen. In fact, when Roxy and I first decided to throw our apartment party, I was shocked to discover I was missing one very important thing I needed: an oven. I called my mom and told her my dilemma. "Whitney," she said with a sigh, "how could you not know you didn't have an oven?" Probably because I never use one! I cook in my toaster oven because it's smaller and easier for just one person. Well, she came up with a great menu for the party that I could do, just using my trusty toaster oven. It can be done, I swear!

Bruschetta

Serves 6–8

1 sourdough baguette (or favorite)
3 red tomatoes finely chopped
Olive oil
Salt and pepper
Parsley or oregano (optional)

Cut half-inch slices of the baguette on the bias. Finely chop all the tomatoes and place in a mixing bowl. Add salt and pepper to taste as well as the parsley/oregano. Mix it all together with olive oil. Brush the sliced bread with olive oil. Put in the toaster oven until crispy. Remove and, while warm, put the marinated tomatoes on top. Ready to serve!

Goat Cheese Phyllo Pouches

Serves 8–10

1 package of phyllo dough
1 log of goat cheese
Olive oil

Defrost the phyllo dough. Take 2–3 pieces and brush the top piece with olive oil. Place one small dollop of goat cheese on dough and fold to look like ravioli. Place pieces in the toaster oven and cook until they are warmed through the center (approx. 12 minutes).

Mini Individual Pizzas

Fresh pizza dough (or frozen)
Tomato sauce (you can use your favorite store-bought one
    such as Giorgio Baldi, but I prefer homemade or just "white")
Shredded mozzarella cheese
Any other toppings you like (e.g., pepperoni slices, peppers, onions, olives)

Go to your local pizza place and buy some freshly made dough. You can also use frozen dough (leave time to defrost) or Boboli. Flatten out your dough, till it's approximately the size of a CD. Make sure to leave a border (about an inch all the way around) for your crust. Pour some marinara sauce on the dough and spread. Top with the mozzarella cheese and any toppings you desire. Toast for 15–20 minutes until dough is cooked and cheese is melted. Serve immediately!

Sit-Down Dinner

I am all about ease, but I believe that a sit-down dinner calls for a little "formality." Don't just put out paper plates and cups; break out the china, even if you don't have a full matching set. Just like I love to mix and match patterns and colors in clothing, I do the same thing with my plates, saucers, and serving dishes. There's nothing wrong with having every setting look different. I've inherited a few pieces from my mom and grandma; others I've picked up for really cheap at flea markets or on sale at places like Z Gallerie, Urban Outfitters, Anthropologie, and Target. You can mix delicate florals with elegant stripes—then put a solid bright bowl or appetizer plate on top. Have fun with it! Same goes for your linens and napkins. All different patterns of florals are cute, too.

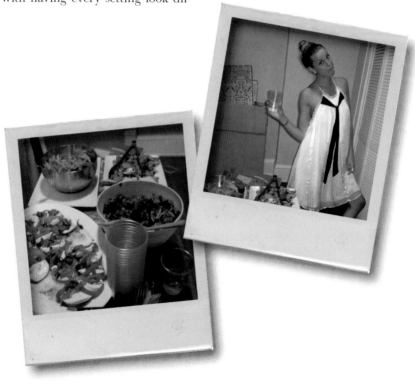

WHITNEY'S TWENTY-FIFTH BIRTHDAY

My twenty-fifth birthday party was held at Cecconi's in West Hollywood last year on Friday, March 12th. The event was designed and planned by BK Events (which is my sis Ashley's company). It wasn't an official surprise, because I knew it was happening, but all Ash told me to do was choose the color palette and show up. The rest she kept under wraps. I wore a white Cinderella-esque Manoush dress with Giuseppe Zanotti heels and Bing Band earrings.

I was one of the first to arrive. It was a very surreal moment, but I embraced it. I felt very lucky to be surrounded by so much love. There is not much more you can ask for at any age. Twenty-five is a big number and comes with a lot of expectations, but if you have support, compassion, and loyalty, everything else is a cakewalk.

My family, Mom, Dad, Ryan, Ashley, Evan, Paige, and my cousin Jackie—every-

one except Jade, who was stuck in Wisconsin at college—was there, as well as my best friends from long, long ago and a couple of new ones. I was so happy that everyone from all walks of my life could spend time together and get to know one another.

The party's design was a modern interpretation of a tea party. The floral arrangements, designed by BK Events and Sticks & Stones, were pink peonies that filled teapots and cups and saucers. The room was candlelit and had a very whimsical feel, complete with accents of pink tulle. Guests sat at two long, supper-style tables.

The menu featured all my faves. As guests arrived there was a small cocktail reception on the outdoor veranda. Guests were served rosé champagne and mini pizzettas on gold-and-white monogrammed cocktail napkins. Inside, the restaurant served ahi tuna tartar followed by a chopped fall vegetable salad. For the entrée, guests had a choice of potato gnocchi, grilled chicken, or branzino. And for dessert (my fave part of the meal!), Ash ordered my favorite birthday cake, that I have every year: the mixed berry cake from Sweet Lady Jane Bakery in L.A.

I'm on my way to the party! I wore a white Manoush dress. The top was fitted and the skirt was a "poof," which kind of matched my favor table.

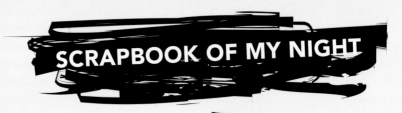
My first look at the decorated room on the night of the party.

The party favor table linen was made out of white tulle and looked like a huge ballerina tutu! Favors were wrapped in pink tissue and pink tulle, and tied with gold foil ribbon. A glittering gold peacock feather was added as an accent.

Guests were seated at two long tables in a private room at a restaurant in West Hollywood. The room is called the Butterfly Room because of the amazing heart and butterfly art hanging in the back.

Each place setting had a hand-calligraphied name card, gold-sequined napkin bands (hand sewn by my sis Ashley), and an Esperance rose to top it off.

The glitter candles were custom ordered and dipped in four tones that flowed with the décor: champagne, almond, gold, and blush.

Turquoise chairs, which are part of the restaurant's design, offset the pink-and-gold theme of my birthday bash. It added a nice pop of color to the candlelit room.

The linens for the party were gold silk underlays with fourteen-karat-gold silk thread embroidery on ivory French lace.

This layout was kind of tricky when it came to seating assignments. Since the room could only hold thirty, there were no bad seats, but separating sixteen and fourteen guests can be hard.

Me and Joanna during the outdoor cocktail portion of the party.

Me and Andrea during dinner.

Me with Sophia.

Packing up at the end of the night.

Brunch

After a tough workweek, there's nothing nicer than getting together with friends on a Saturday or Sunday morning. Call the party for a reasonable hour (around noon) so everyone can sleep in.

Set the mood.

Channel your inner Martha Stewart and make your brunch bright and cheery: whether you serve sit-down or buffet style, everything on the tables should be colorful and feel like a breath of fresh air. Brunches can be casual or fancy, your choice. I prefer to keep it all very low-key (who wants to fuss on a weekend?). I use mismatched glasses in rainbow colors and drape the tables in swags of different fabrics. I even place little decorative pillows on the chairs so people can relax.

Serve up.

Breakfast classics . . . yummy comfort foods that remind everyone of home. You can sprinkle in chocolate chips or fresh fruit in pancakes and top with whipped cream or powdered sugar. But I like my pancakes and waffles "straight up" with warm syrup. Make it easy on yourself if you have a big crowd coming: blend all the dry ingredients and keep in the pantry in Tupperware or a Ziploc bag. All you have to do is add the wet ingredients in the morning and you're ready to start flipping . . .

Tara's Pancakes

Makes 4–6 Pancakes,
Depending on Size

Tara is my mom's best friend and she gave Mom this great recipe. I beg my mom to make these for me whenever I come back home!

1¾ cup flour
1 teaspoon salt
1¾ teaspoons baking powder
3 teaspoons sugar
1 to 1¼ cups milk

2 eggs
6 tablespoons of butter (melted)

In a large bowl, sift together the flour, baking powder, salt, and sugar. Pour in the milk, eggs, and melted butter; mix until smooth. Heat a lightly oiled griddle or frying pan over medium-high heat. Pour or scoop the batter onto the griddle, using approximately ¼ cup for each pancake. Brown on both sides and serve hot.

Belgian Waffles

Makes 8 Small Squares or 2 Large Belgian Waffles

My mom is a master at making these. I always liked them filled with chocolate chips!

1 ¾ cup flour
1 tablespoon sugar
1 egg
1 ½ cup beer (not light)
¼ cup oil
1 teaspoon vanilla

Mix all ingredients and allow to stand for two hours or more at room temp. Grease waffle iron before using.

Frozen Bellini

½ cup peach nectar or purée
¼ cup peach schnapps
Crushed ice
¾ cup chilled champagne or Prosecco

Mix all ingredients in a blender until smooth. Pour into champagne flutes and garnish with a peach. Cheers!

A Dessert Party

This is a fun twist on a potluck dinner: you make the main meal, and ask guests to BYOD (bring your own dessert)—enough for everyone. Sweet! Of course, you'll want to make a few of your own treats to set the bar high . . . I love the idea of creating a sundae buffet with all the fixin's (M&Ms, gummy bears, crushed graham crackers, crushed Oreos, chocolate chips, sprinkles, chopped nuts, shredded coconut, etc.) or minitarts (just buy some mini premade pie crusts, top with chunks of apple, pear, or peaches, and bake) à la mode.

The right light.

Everything looks better in dim lighting. A really cheap way to make your space more inviting is by installing a dimmer on your regular lighting switch. You don't even have to be an electrician to be able to do this; all you need is a screwdriver. Or, of course, if you're using all lamps like I used to, get some lower-watt bulbs, or try a sheer piece of fabric over a few of the shades to set the mood. Turn the lights down low and light some candles when it's time for the final course of the meal.

Lay it all out.

After the dinner, prepare a pretty, large, buffet-style table to display everyone's goodies. Make sure you have plenty of small plates (glass or see-through plastic ones are great; they won't distract from the decadent desserts!) and serving forks/spoons. I like to go around the room and ask who brought what and what the story is behind each dessert.

Fudge Nut Sauce

Makes 2 Cups

This is my mom's decadent creation! I pour it on top of coffee ice cream. Yum! It's ultraimpressive; it actually hardens as it cools. I keep the leftovers in a Tupperware container in the fridge, then pop it into the microwave and use it for dipping fruit.

> ½ pound butter or margarine (2 sticks)
> 1 (12 oz.) package semisweet Nestlé chocolate chips
> 1 cup coarsely chopped walnuts or pecans (optional)

In a double boiler over hot (not boiling) water, melt butter or margarine and chocolate chips, stirring until smooth. Stir in nuts. Serve hot. May be refrigerated and reheated.

Hamantaschen

Makes 2 Dozen Cookies

A classic Jewish pastry! It's served on the holiday of Purim—which is kind of like Halloween, because you get to dress up in costumes but it's in the winter. I actually love hamantaschen for breakfast with coffee, so I make it any time of year. Purim celebrates the Jews' freedom from Haman—an evil guy with a signature accessory: his large, triangular-shaped hat. So that's why the pastry is a triangular shape, the shape of Haman's hat. I just love food that incorporates fashion!

> 2 cups flour
> ½ pound butter
> 2 (8 oz.) packages cream cheese

1 jar jam/jelly (my mom uses the traditional apricot or
    raspberry, but you can use your favorite)
1 egg (yolk only)
Chopped nuts (optional)

Combine the first three ingredients and refrigerate (overnight recommended). Roll dough to nice workable thickness, about ¼ inch thick. Cut circles 3 inches in diameter. Put ¼ teaspoon of your favorite jam or jelly in center of each circle. You may add nuts. Moisten edges with egg yolk. Pinch corners to form a triangle. Bake at 375 degrees for 10 minutes.

Wendy's Fudge

My aunt Wendy taught me how to make this, and trust me, there is never enough. If you get invited somewhere at the last minute, don't panic, this is a great hostess gift!

4 cups chocolate chips
4 cups mini marshmallows
1 cup peanut butter (crunchy)

Melt chocolate bits in a microwave or a double boiler for 1 minute. Stir and repeat at 20-second intervals until melted. Spray a rubber spatula with a nonstick cooking spray and stir in peanut butter. Fold in marshmallows and stir until covered with chocolate. Pour into a 9-by-13-inch foil-lined pan. Chill in refrigerator for at least 15–20 minutes until hardened. Lift out foil and cut with a pizza wheel into bite-size pieces.

Drink up.

A sweet signature cocktail for the evening! To garnish, dip the rim of the glass in cocoa powder or drop an unwrapped Hershey's Kiss into the drink.

Vodka Espresso

This can be served instead of coffee!

1oz. vodka
½ oz. Godiva mocha liqueur
1 oz. cold espresso
1 splash simple syrup

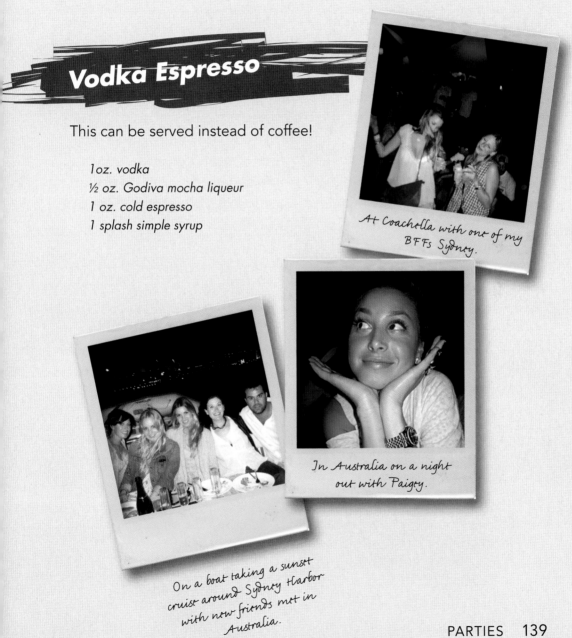

At Coachella with one of my BFFs Sydney.

In Australia on a night out with Paigey.

On a boat taking a sunset cruise around Sydney Harbor with new friends met in Australia.

GUESTS GONE WILD

Practically every bash I have thrown or attended had a few of these types. Recently, a girl at one of my parties got really drunk and hit on Roxy's boyfriend (I could see the steam coming out of Rox's ears). Here's how to handle unruly guests.

The lush.

She's been doing shots of Jägermeister all night and has now fallen facedown in your fondue pot. She's drunk as a skunk and still begging for more booze.

What to do: Offer to call her a cab and get her home before she hurls; if she drove, make sure you take her car keys.

The slut.

In just a few hours, she's made out with your coworker and your brother, and now she's organizing a game of strip poker.

What to do: Kindly tell her to keep her clothes on. But unless she's offended anyone (chances are none of the guys will be complaining), there's little you can do about her "friendliness." If she's really annoying you, ask her to leave. She'll prob-ably be happy to take one of her boy toys home for the night.

The loudmouth.

His comments are rude, lewd, and giving you a throbbing headache. This blowhard can't keep his opinions to himself or his voice down to a dull roar.

What to do: Be as direct as he is: explain that you have neighbors and he has to take it down a notch or leave the premises. If he doesn't get the message . . . try using a whistle.

The leech.

She's glued to your side, barely letting you spend a minute with any of your other guests.

What to do: This clinging vine is probably just feeling insecure. Does she know anyone else at the party? Is she shy? Make introductions and try to find her someone she has something in common with to talk to. If all else fails, ask a kind friend to "babysit" her for a few minutes so you can get a break.

LAST-MINUTE PARTIES

It was a weekend and I was bored . . . so on a totally Whitney whim, I decided, "Let's have a party!" I called a few friends who were free and they said they'd be over in a few hours. Which left me wondering . . . "WHAT HAVE I DONE?"

The first thing to do is make a list—that way you can see what you are up against. Also, don't be proud and think you have to cook everything yourself. Order in. I even found a place right in SoHo that delivers gourmet bite-size cupcakes for dessert

This is one of the best parts of living on your own; you don't have to ask anyone's permission to throw a party. You just do it!

After I calmed down, I realized this wasn't a reason to stress. This is one of the best parts of living on your own; you don't have to ask anyone's permission to throw a party. You just do it! With a little ingenuity—and a few takeout menus—I knew I could pull it off.

I do have to warn you, though, to keep a last-minute party small and manageable; that means five to ten guests, not fifty. Not only do you have to coordinate your entire event, but you have to figure out what you are going to wear, do your hair, and so on.

(bakedbymelissa.com). There's also nothing wrong with phoning your local supermarket, deli, Chinese takeout, or pizza place and asking them to put together a few platters. Break out the china; it makes even a slice of pepperoni look pretty. Have everyone bring a bottle of wine, and you're all set. Instant soiree!

Because my sis has her own party-planning biz (BK Events, bkevents.net), she's the perfect person to answer all my questions about cooking, serving, and hostessing.

Whitney: Should you tell people where to sit at the dinner table?

Ashley: This all depends on how many guests you are entertaining. If you have a lot of bodies—and a few tables—placecards can help prevent people from getting "stuck" next to someone they don't know/like. On the flip side, you can also "place" people together—which is great if you're trying to fix up two friends! But if it's a really casual dinner with only a few folks, there's really no need for that. Let everyone take a seat where they're comfortable. There are many nontraditional ways to make seating cards, too. You don't have to be superformal. You can write names on something cute—like a napkin ring or even in icing on a piece of chocolate!

Whitney: What if you make a dish . . . and someone tells you they don't eat what you're serving? Should I ask people what they will/won't eat?

Ashley: If you are entertaining at home, you should always have a vegetarian option as part of the menu. This way, if guests don't like the main dish, they don't go hungry! A simple soup or a salad is great; or some roasted veggies/potatoes to accompany the entree. Otherwise, you don't need to "clear" the menu beforehand—unless you have a guest of honor, and you want to celebrate him/her by making a favorite dish.

Whitney: What do you do if you burn dinner right before the party?

Ashley: Obviously, it's important to make a timeline for cooking. That way if you make mistakes, you can always redo a dish. But if the situation does arise—and your guests are at the door—call for delivery! Your guests will understand and it makes for a good laugh later.

Whitney: Do I have to serve red wine with meat? Can I serve it with chicken or fish?

Ashley: For years people have believed you needed to serve white with chicken and fish, and red with steak. You don't have to stick to those *exact* rules, but it's important to keep a balance between food and wine. You want to make sure one doesn't overpower the other. If you are serving a heavy dish, you would need a richer or stronger wine to complement it. Likewise, a lighter entree would need a softer wine. I suggest a red with beef or lamb, but if you want to switch it up and serve a red with fish or chicken, go with a pinot noir. It's a lighter red.

WHITTYISM: WHEN YOU'RE THE GUEST

You don't want to show up empty-handed. Most people bring the party host/hostess a bottle of wine, a box of chocolates . . . *boring*. I like to give something a bit more out of the box! If the host is an old friend, how about a scrapbook or wine-of-the-month club membership. It's also fun to bring a board game for all to play, like Taboo or Scattergories. Bake something: I often bring someone their fave dessert—my best friend, Joanna, loves this chocolate chip banana bread that my mom bakes so I wrap up a loaf for her. I think playlists are also great gifts. I like to make a CD and bring it to pop on at the party. Or—if unusual is what you're after—how about some whimsical trash bags? Findgift.com has some wacky ones printed with goldfish; tell your host they come with an offer to help her clean up after the gang has cleared out.

CHAPTER FIVE

DATING

Everyone always says—my mom included—you have to kiss a lot of frogs before you find your prince. She wasn't kidding; I have locked lips with loads of toads. But that's okay, because dating—really putting yourself out there and being open to new people, new relationships—is the only way to figure out what and who you want.

Dating in your twenties is very different from dating in your college years. When you're an adult, it feels like suddenly everyone is looking for a "serious" relationship. There's pressure to settle down, to couple off, to not be "the last one" of your girlfriends to get engaged. But sometimes it's hard to distinguish Mr. Right from Mr. "Great Body, Well-Dressed, but Forgets to Call on Saturday." Although I don't believe you have to lasso the first guy who seems like "marriage material," I do think you have to consider the kind of person you want to be with for the long run. Don't necessarily rule out all the others (they can be fun, even if they're not your perfect match, and teach you what you do and don't want or what you can or cannot handle), but at least start to think about yourself—your needs, your desires, your goals—and how someone else might fit into that picture.

Dating on a reality TV show is even *more* complicated. Most people have to deal with their pals fixing them up—I also have to deal with my producers playing matchmaker! On a recent photo shoot, one of them asked me to "check out" the photographer (who was apparently checking me out the entire time). He was French; he was artsy; he drove a motorcycle—they thought he'd be a good guy for me. Truthfully, I didn't feel any electricity between us on the shoot, but I said, "Sure . . . why not?" I always trust my first impression. Rarely am I surprised, but it's worth giving guys a chance. I think it's fine to meet a guy for drinks or a coffee—even if you don't think it's going to amount to much. It's a few hours out of your life; if you're truly not into it, then keep it quick. That takes a lot of the pressure off.

Like almost everything in life, relationships are all about trial and error. My old roommate Erin used to tell me to play the field; that's what dating is about. She'd say, "You go out, you see a couple of people, then you see some people less and less . . . until you wind up exclusive, if that's what you want." I wish it were that easy!

Love can happen when you least expect it, as long as you're open to the experience. So accept the invitations, take chances, and enjoy yourself! It can be a lot of fun if you're willing to go on a few fix-ups or have some flings, with the only expectation that this is going to be *interesting*.

I grew up reading fairy tales, where shining knights on white horses ride in and sweep princesses off their feet. I don't know if I believe those stories (Prince Charming better hurry up—my feet are killing me!), but I do believe in love. I believe that two people can share an incredible, deep, once-in-this-lifetime connection

Accept the invitations, take chances, and enjoy yourself!

and commitment to each other. I believe love isn't just about lust (though that part is certainly fun); it's about caring deeply about someone. I also think friendship has to play a big part. Your partner, your husband, your significant other—whomever he/she is should also be your best friend, your confidant, your support system. That person should love you for you, for every little quirk and craziness that drives other people up a wall. When you find that someone . . . you know. My wise married sis, Ashley, always tells me you should never settle, and be totally prepared to be vulnerable.

That said, I also don't feel you need a man in your life to make you complete. There's nothing wrong with being single! My family raised me to be an independent woman (although when I go home my sisters are always looking after me). I know there are plenty of ladies out there who feel totally lost without a love in their life. I don't feel this way at all. I'm okay being single in the city. And trust me, that's much more attractive to a guy than a girl who reeks of desperation. It is also so much more empowering to be alone than to stay in a dysfunctional relationship purely because it's comfortable.

I have been in four major relationships in my life: a high school boyfriend who I was on and off with for a couple years; a college boyfriend who was my first "true love"; my first romance in NYC (a certain Australian rocker!), which quickly turned into a relationship; and a more mature relationship filled with compassion and vulnerability. I would love to take certain qualities from all my boyfriends and mesh them together to make the perfect man. But I know "perfect" is only a figment of one's imagination. Still, if I could take my first boyfriend's empathy and ability to listen, pair it with my second boyfriend's humor and charm, mix it up with my rocker boy-

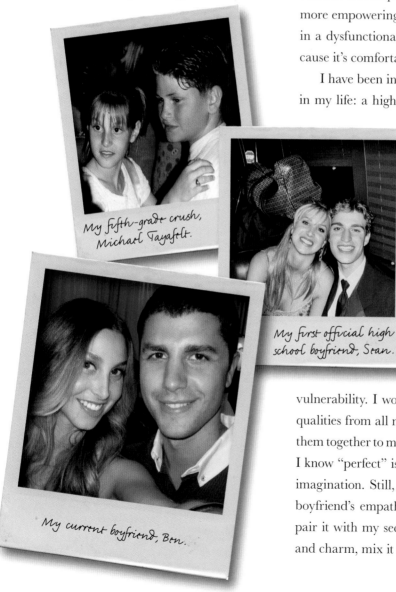

My fifth-grade crush, Michael Tayafolt.

My first official high school boyfriend, Sean.

My current boyfriend, Ben.

friend's passion and compassion, and then mesh them with my last boyfriend's sensitivity and depth . . . well, that would be one fabulous guy. Dream on, huh?

You know all those books they write about guys and girls being from separate planets? There's a reason. We women try looking for love—Jay in particular. I had just moved to NYC, and by *just* I mean I met him literally during my first weekend here when I interviewed at DVF. He was performing at a local bar, and it just happened. We were filming that night, so the cameras were able to catch it all (lucky

It is also so much more empowering to be alone than to stay in a dysfunctional relationship purely because it's comfortable.

to figure out what makes a man tick—and what makes a relationship stick. Boys are so confusing! Sometimes you want to slap them and say, "Can't you just tell me how you feel?" However, they think of us in the same light.

My sister Ashley just got married to an amazing guy, Evan Bogart. When I asked her how she knew he was the one, she said, "He was everything I never knew I was really looking for in a man. Of course he had the qualities that every woman fantasizes about, but he was also kind, honest, funny, a good communicator, cute, ambitious, creative, and devoted."

My previous boyfriends all turned into "something more" at times when I wasn't us!). I took the bull by the horns and offered to buy Jay a drink after his set. We were instantly enthralled in conversation and spent the whole night dancing until I had to leave for the airport at 6:00 A.M. The time just flew by.

I had heard that New York was the place to date around 'cause men abound! But soon, I found myself in the midst of an intense relationship, on and off camera! In the few years before, while filming *The Hills*, I never let my old boyfriend be filmed. I just wanted to keep part of my life private, and now I know why it was so important. A real romance cannot survive being documented on a reality TV series. You never quite let your guard down, and you're never 100 percent honest about how you're feeling, because you're always thinking, *I can't say that because everyone is watching.*

Love is between two people; it's meant to be private.

I will never (let me say it again!) NEVER allow a serious boyfriend to be part of the show. I've learned it's a recipe for disaster. Love is between two people; it's meant to be private. You don't always know guys' motives, and to have all these opinions of strangers as well as a crew weighing in becomes too much of a burden. It totally takes the spontaneity out of a relationship. I will certainly go on dates, but if any guy I meet turns out to be someone I really want to give my heart to . . . I'm keeping him as far from the cameras as possible!

My final love lesson is communication. It's key. I feel like it's been the biggest hurdle I have had to overcome in all of my relationships, and I think a lot of girls feel this way. I always assume the man I'm dating knows precisely what I'm thinking, what I want, what is right and what is wrong, but he doesn't! *Hmmm* . . . you mean men aren't mind readers? Ladies, we have to *tell* them. We have to open up and be honest and say what we think is great and working in the relationship, and what is out of whack or just plain pissing us off. It cracks me up, because I (and most girls in general) can gab for hours with my girlfriends, analyzing every nuance of our relationships. But when it comes to a guy I'm actually involved with? I zip my lip and hope he has psychic abilities. One of the things I really need to work on is allowing myself to open up and be vulnerable.

When you want to give your guy something sweet, try one of the incredible flavors from Baked by Melissa.

WHITTYISM: GUY-WOWING GIFTS

Relationships are stressful enough . . . then comes Hanukkah, Christmas, Valentine's Day, his birthday. You can't just get your guy *any* gift. It has to show how much you know about him; it has to say "I'm the coolest, best girlfriend in the world and you are *so* lucky to have me." I have found that these gifts are definitely man-pleasers and will earn you brownie points for creativity! An added plus—they won't break your bank account.

- A DIY cupcake. Bake him a pair (one for you/one for him), then provide a "palette" of his fave toppings: chocolate frosting, whipped cream, M&Ms, Reeses, gummy worms . . . you name it. Tell him you chose this present because he's "so sweet."
- What hardworking man wouldn't love a massage . . . by you? Make it as spalike an experience as possible: dim the lights, put on soothing music, sprinkle rose petals around the room, and rub him with scented oil.
- Break out the video camera (you can ask a good friend to help if you don't have a tripod) and record him a sexy music video. Can't carry a tune? He won't notice, especially if you belt out "I'm Too Sexy" or do your best Britney impression of "Baby One More Time." He'll beg for an encore for sure!
- Play some naughty versions of childhood games. A friend of mine bought her boyfriend Twister . . . then told him they had to play it in the buff! If you're not quite as bold, there's always spin the bottle!
- Beer-of-the-month club membership. He'll think of you with every brew!
- A sweet, heartfelt note. Simple yes, but you'll wow him with your honesty and admiration. What guy wouldn't love a love letter?
- A scent. Kind of a selfish gift, but men always appreciate cologne.

MEET THE PARENTS

For some people, introducing their new boyfriend/girlfriend to their folks is no big deal. But I need a little preparation. Like the time I was on just date number two with Freddie Facklemayer. (I had met Freddie through his brother, Harry, who had invited Freddie out with us.) Freddie seemed like a nice New York boy and he was also a friend of my friend Sami. But then he surprised me by asking his dad along to dinner—when we barely knew each other. He felt totally comfortable with the introduction in the early stages of our relationship; I, on the other hand, broke out in a cold sweat. I just wasn't ready to meet his dad!

Most people feel that "meeting the parents" is a big step. It says that you're serious; you want your family to like and accept him, and you want his parents to think you're the greatest thing since Spanx. Although it's hard to know when it's the right time (that really depends on how you feel), generally three months is a good amount of time to wait before making introductions. When the time arrives—and you're face-to-face with his folks . . .

- Make sure you're dressed conservatively (not too sexy). Avoid skintight clothing, plunging necklines—basically anything sloppy or slutty. They'll be looking you over from head to toe, so make sure you're polished and put together.

- Even if your knees are knocking, be friendly and warm and try to at least look at ease. Be yourself; don't put on airs or act like someone you think they want you to be. Your integrity will impress them.

- Ask polite questions. People love to talk about themselves. Like, "I love this painting in the family room. Where did you find it?" An added plus: you'll learn lots about your boyfriend's past (maybe even details about his former girlfriends!).

- If you're going to his family's home for a meal or for an overnight, bring a token gift. Anything! A bottle of wine, a bunch of flowers, a small dessert. One summer, I went to visit my boyfriend's home in Martha's Vineyard. I knew I would be the guest of his family, and I couldn't come empty-handed. I brought some bubble-wrapped bud vases in my suitcase. When I left, I placed them in their kitchen while everyone was sleeping (I had to leave and make an early flight home). It was *very* appreciated! I also recently bought a guy friend's mom an awesome new Italian cookbook. You can never have enough cookbooks!

THE L WORD

This was a huge debate between me, Erin Lucas, and Jay: When is the right time to say "I love you" in a relationship? Erin's guy, Duncan, blurted it out before she did—and after a mere two weeks. Jay said he thinks people say it too quickly. His theory is you wait and see if it's *really* love (as opposed to infatuation). My take is if it feels right, it *is* right—no matter what the timing is for anyone else. Some guys might get scared. But what if he feels the same way? What if he's holding back on saying it to you because he fears your reaction? I say go for it, girl! There are so many great ways to say it! You don't have to make a big production out of it; just look into his eyes . . . and say it. Of course, there are cuter and more eloquent ways—like spelling out "I Love You" in jelly beans on the bed or writing it in lipstick on his bathroom mirror. Some people get all poetic—but usually that's just in the movies.

Here is one of my favorite "I love you" lines from a flick (in case you need a little inspiration):

I love that you get cold when it's seventy-one degrees out. I love that it takes you an hour and a half to order a sandwich. I love that you get a little crinkle above your nose when you're looking at me like I'm nuts. I love that after I spend the day with you, I can still smell your perfume on my clothes. And I love that you are the last person I want to talk to before I go to sleep at night.

—Billy Crystal in *When Harry Met Sally*

A GUY'S PERSPECTIVE: WHITNEY'S BEST BOY BUD, BEN

Ben and I have known each other for over a decade. We went to school together from seventh grade through sophomore year of college at the University of Colorado-Boulder, when I transferred to USC. We are constantly analyzing the opposite sex with each other; he thinks girls are crazy and I think guys are crazier! Sometimes he'll call and leave me a message, "Whit, I need your advice in the love department . . ." I do enjoy hearing his trials and tribulations, and I often ask him for insights into the male mind.

Ben's such a great friend. We are constantly gushing about our romantic endeavors/issues to each other.

For example, I knew a guy in college who was relentless; he asked me out in every virtual way possible . . . on Facebook, via text and IM, and on and on . . . Ben warned me about this guy. He said it was a bad sign that he was this desperate at the beginning, so I should probably just nip it in the bud right away. But I didn't listen. And after much effort on his part, I finally gave in to Mr. Cyberstalker (mostly because he invited me to a Bob Dylan concert and there was no way I could pass that up). After the date, in which we didn't say a word to each other for basically the whole concert, I called Ben immediately and told him I should have listened to him to begin with. From then on, I have always trusted Ben's relationship advice. I know he'll tell it to me straight.

Whitney: So how do you know if she's "the one"?

Ben: I don't think any guy really knows unless that girl turns into his wife. Most guys are afraid to answer that question or even think about "the one." I'm sweating just thinking about it! I think after a long time of being together and getting comfortable with each other, you can start to tell if you can be with a certain girl for the long-term.

Whitney: Why do guys do stupid things?

Ben: I wish I could answer that. Guys do stupid things just like girls do stupid things. We're all crazy. When emotions become involved, people can act irrationally—male or female. As much as we'd like to believe we're grown-ups, we're still learning how to behave and treat each other.

Whitney: Sex on the first date . . . yay or nay? Does a guy think any differently of a girl who hooks up that quickly?

Ben: It depends. If I honestly feel like there is something special with a certain girl, and I see potential for us having a future together, I think the smartest thing to do is wait and take it slow. A guy may think differently about a girl who hooks up quickly. But I think it really depends on the guy. Personally, if a girl hooks up quickly, I don't automatically think she is a slut. But depending on other things, it may add to that assumption.

WHITNEY 101: SIX SIGNS IT'S GETTING SERIOUS

You know how you feel, and you *think* he's ready to commit. Here's how to be sure:

1 He calls you his "girlfriend."

Especially when he introduces you to "important" people—like his college frat brothers, bandmates, or bosses. And when he says it, he doesn't choke on the word. He actually smiles! And instead of "I" or "me" he's talking "we."

2 He asks your opinion.

He values what you think of his tie or his new Web site design. He even wants to know who you think will win the Super Bowl (even if you don't follow football!). This shows that he respects you.

3 He's willing to make sacrifices.

If something is important to you, then it's important to him. Like when I asked Jay to come to Olivia's "Socials" dinner party. At first, he said no. But then he showed up—which showed me he cared more about me than just hanging out with his friends.

4 He gets green with envy.

This happens every time you mention, text, or even look at another guy. I remember how freaked out Jay got when I told him I had lunch with my workmate Chris (smooth move on my part!). If even purely platonic relationships make him jealous, it indicates he wants you all to himself.

5 He's fast-forwarding to the future.

All of a sudden, he's quizzing you about how you see your future: Do you want to be married in a church or by Elvis in Vegas? House in the burbs or apartment in the city? How many kids? These aren't just hypotheticals or small talk; he's thinking long term and making sure you're on the same page. He's also trying to gauge your reaction—or what you're doing on a certain date within the next couple months.

6 He wants to be with you.

Every chance he gets! And he sacrifices his own time to be with you.

WOULD I LIE TO YOU, BABE?

Honesty is *everything* in a relationship. If there's no trust, you'll crumble as a couple. Of course, I had to find this out for myself the hard way: like when both Alex, a guy I once dated, and my friend Jess both warned me that Jay wasn't being honest about his ex, Danielle. Jay was staying with me, but coming home at five or six in the morning, and I didn't know where he was. Shouldn't I have seen the writing on the wall? Shouldn't I have figured out he was hooking up with his ex again? Part of me didn't want to admit this to myself; sometimes, it's just easier to put blinders on and not acknowledge the problems.

So how do you know if your guy lies? A lot of it is trusting your own instincts. Kelly Cutrone always says, "The truth doesn't always come like a shiny little bluebird on someone's shoulder." Sometimes you just have this feeling in the pit of your stomach. Oprah has her *aha!* moments. Well, I have my *uh-oh!* moments. These are the times a little bell goes off in the back of my brain and it tells me, "Whitney . . . wise up. Something is not right here." Unfortunately, I don't always listen. So now—sadder but wiser—here's my advice for you. Listen to your own inner voice. Don't be paranoid or accusative until you have evidence, but *do* be smart. Sometimes guys are really good at covering up what they've been up to. Jay certainly was slick in that department. But I had begun to feel a tension between us; the passion was kind of waning. And when we'd talk over dinner or drinks, and I'd tell him what a bad day at work I had, he didn't seem to care. He didn't really even seem interested. I could see his eyes avoiding mine. Telltale sign right there: if he can't look you in the eye, he's definitely hiding something from you.

When you do finally clear the air and get things out in the open, it probably won't be pretty. Jay got superdefensive when I asked him why he couldn't be honest with me. But you can't keep quiet forever because you're afraid of rocking the boat. If someone is lying to you, he doesn't respect you or care about you in a way that you deserve.

THE EX FILES

So over—that's what I thought it was with Jay. He was off on tour, out of my life, and I was just trying to move on. Then he shows up outside the DVF store during an event to tell me he's sorry and he felt bad with how we ended things. Then came the inevitable: "Whit, I made a mistake . . ." Translation: let's get back together. Forgive and forget and take me back, why don't ya? It was tempting; I had obviously been missing him, and he caught me off guard. Plus, he looked *really* hot in that black suit with that scruffy beard. He even had tears in his eyes when he said, "I love you. Better late than never . . ." I stood my ground; I told him it was too little, too late. And I meant it. I'm not the kind of girl who crumbles. When I make a decision, I stick to it—even if I wasn't 100 percent sure that he cheated.

Jay's so cute (and also has the sweetest soul). He really got me through my first year in NYC.

I know it's *so* easy to go back to someone you were once with. You have to weigh the pros and the cons: What was good about the relationship? What was bad? What needs to change and what will *never* change? What do you want in your life—and is he really a part of that picture?

Before you indulge in a blast from your past, consider this:

The reason you split.

Why did you break up in the first place? What were the issues you had, and have they been resolved? Has he really changed—or can you live with things you couldn't live with before? Make a list; check it twice.

Your head as well as your heart.

If you're swept up in emotion ("He's back! He's back!"), it's hard to see clearly. Before you agree to rekindle your relationship, give yourself time to think things through.

Your expectations for the future.

Do you think getting back together is a long-term commitment? Or are you just looking for a fun flashback?

WHITNEY 101: SIX SIGNS IT'S OVER

If your relationship is experiencing several of these, honey, you're history . . .

1 Absence is making the heart grow colder.

You should be able to be apart for a night or even a few days and not worry his eye (and God knows what else) is wandering. Like the time my friend Allie went on a modeling assignment and her longtime live-in boyfriend, Adam, kissed another girl. Freedom should not equal a free pass to fool around behind your back.

2 The fire has fizzled.

You can't remember the last time the two of you kissed, cuddled, fooled around, did *anything* besides argue.

3 You have nothing to say.

Literally. You stare across the table from each other at dinner, and the conversation is tense and strained. It probably should have clued me in when all Jay and I had to talk about was work, weather, and how wonderful he was.

MY HAIR-STORY

My hair and I have had a love-hate relationship. One of the most stressful tress moments happened when I was about fifteen. I decided I wanted to go blonder, so I used one of those at-home coloring kits and left it on just a *little* too long. When I came out of the bathroom, my sister Paige gasped in horror: my hair was orange. Not a lovely Lindsay Lohan auburn red . . . that would have been tolerable. I'm talking Sunny Delight orange. Hideous. I couldn't even get an appointment at the salon to fix it for several days, so I wore a hat to school, hoping no one would notice.

Over the years, my hair has been dozens of different shades, shapes, and lengths—all in my endless quest to land on a style that I love. I was born with kind of the same hair I have now—fairly straight strawberry blond with a little curl on the bottom. When I was in high school, it was "the blonder, the better." I wanted to look like a real beach blonde. In 2006, I cut it off to my chin—the second-hugest hair mistake in my life.

In college my hair was mostly long and blond—except for a few months where I decided chocolate brown would look good on me (it didn't; it turned green). When I look back on early episodes of *The Hills,* my hair in my sophomore year was one solid mass of platinum blond. Thankfully, I'm over that phase; it took me nearly two years to get back to my natural shade, and I am so grateful to my colorist Johnny Ramirez at Chris McMillan Salon in L.A. for painstakingly working in natural highlights and lowlights and bringing my hair back to a state of healthy shininess again. It's important to find a stylist you love and trust—he should be your "Mr. Right" of Hair. He/ she should hear you and not try to force his/her "vision" on you. For years, I felt like the stylists I was using just didn't get what I was saying: "Guys, I want my hair to look real!" Finally, Johnny listened—and he assured me he'd grant my hair wish, if I was patient and let him

do it in baby steps (you can't erase years of bleaching trauma overnight).

These days, my hair is pretty long, thick, and wavy. I love the length and want to grow it even longer—but it's not low maintenance. Long hair knots easily and can get fried from coloring, styling, and sitting in the sun. Through much trial and error—and my hair paying the price—I have finally settled on a hair-care regimen that I like and that works for me. I love Enjoy Luxury shampoo and conditioner. It comes in hot pink bottles (very me!), and my cousin Jackie Braverman is a stylist in Vegas and sends me big tubs of it. I get my hair done so frequently for the show, dates, and appearances, the hot tools annihilate my hair. These products make it feel so soft and healthy again. I also use Frédéric Fekkai protein cream. I brush it through my hair and douse it on the tips at night before I fall asleep. It just sinks in, and when I wake up in the morning, my hair feels reborn! I also just got this Mason Pearson boar paddle brush, which was really pricey, but a good investment. The natural bristles polish the hair, laying

personal—as personal as picking your own wardrobe. There are some general guidelines you can follow, based on hair type (see the next section), but in the end, you should settle on what makes your hair feel healthy, shiny, bouncy, and so on. I say experiment! If someone gives me a new product or I see a small sample bottle at the drugstore, I'll give it a whirl. It may not do wonders for my hair . . . but then again, it could be the magic potion I've been searching for.

the cuticle flat to make the hair shine—and it doesn't tear my hair out like some hard vinyl bristle brushes do. And I just found a great new product: Moroccan oil. It's a great leave-in conditioner that smells good, and a little goes a long way.

The important thing is to find products that work for your hair—not for your roomie, your mother, or that A-lister who flaunts her fabulous mane in ads. It's very

WHITNEY 101: WHAT'S MY TYPE?

Every hair has a type. Mine is "normal," meaning I can go a few days without washing before it gets greasy. Here's a quick guide to the basics and how to best handle your hair's condition:

Oily Hair

Hair looks slightly dull and "dirty," especially at the scalp, and strands feel slippery when you run your fingers over them. Your tresses tend to be limp and stringy and feel "weighed down."

How to treat it:

Shampoo more often, at least every other day, with a shampoo for oily hair. Maybe every other wash skip the conditioner.

Dry Hair

Hair looks frizzy, or flyaway, almost like straw. If the scalp is also dry, you can also have dandruff flakes (no fun!).

How to treat it:

Shampoo three times a week (any more and you'll make it even dryer) with a moisturizing shampoo, and always condition—even if you're just giving hair a rinse. If hair is superdry, you can use a leave-in conditioner as well (a lighter one for day and a deep-conditioning cream on ends at night). Avoid products that contain alcohol, since this can dry hair out even more.

Combination Hair

As the day goes on, your hair starts to look oily around the roots, but the ends remain dry.

How to treat it:

Shampoo every other day with a shampoo for normal hair and concentrate on the scalp. Use a conditioner, but only on the ends. Use dry shampoo in place of regular every other wash. Oscar Blandi makes a great one.

Normal Hair

If your hair is neither oily nor dry, you'll want to just keep your hair clean, conditioned, and protected.

How to treat it:

Shampoo three to four times a week with a gentle shampoo. Follow with conditioner on the ends or a leave-in conditioner.

HAIR SPEAK

Someone should have warned me that coif communication does not come naturally. There were times in the past when I was doing a shoot and I'd say "I want a romantic updo" and I'd wind up looking like Marge Simpson! I've since learned that with a few simple strategies for speaking to a stylist, you can get *exactly* what you want:

- Make a list of what you are looking for in a hairstyle. Is it versatility? A look that's professional and easy to care for? Something elegant for a special occasion? Write down a list of adjectives to describe your ideal look: sexy, sophisticated, chic, and so on. And bring inspirational pics!

- Be realistic about the style you are choosing. Are you asking for a straight hairstyle when you have really curly hair? The stylist is good . . . but he or she can't work miracles.

- The words *trim* or *cut* mean different things to different people. Rather than say "trim my hair," show the length of hair you'd like cut with your fingers when hair is *dry* or give the stylist a measurement: "Take off an inch only" or "Just the ends, please." I am so crazy about haircuts. Be sure to trim hair every couple of months so it stays healthy.

- Discuss your daily routine with the stylist so the person understands what your needs are. Are you willing to spend twenty minutes blow-drying every morning when you have to be at work by eight? Or do you just want to brush and go in the morning?

- Let the stylist know your hair's particular challenges: Is it hard to curl? Does it fall flat easily? Get oily in the afternoon? This may influence the cut he/she gives and can also help the stylist give you advice.

- Check out celeb and hair magazines and tear out lots of pictures of styles you like. You can then say, "I want to look like this," or choose the whispy bangs from one, the length from another, and the sides from yet another picture. Sometimes, a pic is worth a thousand words.

- Before the stylist begins snipping, have him tell you what he heard you say, and make sure you're on the same page.

WHITTYISM: CHEAP CUTS

If you want to go to a really nice salon—and you can't afford the sky-high price of the famous top stylist—ask to book an appointment with the stylist's assistant. The assistants usually do cuts for half the price, and they've worked under the top person, so they have learned from the best. And because they're still climbing the ladder (like you!), they're eager to please and will really spend the time listening to you and working on your hair.

SPECIAL OCCASION DOS

My stylist from Rare NYC, Charles Strahan, always tells me that a woman's style should reflect her "authenticity of style," meaning what kind of person she truly is: pretty, punk, edgy, classic, cool, and so on. It's important to know who is inside, even if you are going for a look that is somewhat of a departure. So even if I am doing heavy metal chic for an MTV event, Charles gives my hair a slightly softer spin on rock and roll—because he knows, in my heart, I'm no bad girl! We called one look "Pretty Punk Ballerina." My dress was black and had unfinished and rough textures, my eyes were smoky with vibrant color, and my hair was rough textured but pulled into a large low bun. It felt cutting-edge and cool . . . but I didn't feel like I was in disguise. It still felt like me.

I like my hair to appear soft and touchable and never *too* perfect . . . sometimes we might play up my waves but keep them natural looking; sometimes we make it rougher, sometimes curlier, sometimes more structured. The differences are subtle, but my hair rarely looks the same for an event—and we always have *fun*!

When it comes to styling hair for a party or special occasion, it's important to take into account the vibe of the party (Is it formal? Funky? Casual?), the time of year/day, and of course, what you're wearing. The shape and silhouette of your outfit has to work with your hair; the texture or the fabric should relate to the texture of your hair.

Andrea (my BFF) braided my hair in two French braids, and then I put the ends up in a bun.

UPDO HOW-TOS

Charles knows how much I like to be creative and mix things up a bit—so when I sit down for a styling session for an event, he'll say, "What are we gonna do to stop traffic tonight?" These are not your ordinary updos; I think they feel fresh and fun, not frumpy. The other great part is that they take virtually no time to style (a good thing because I'm often running behind schedule!) and they stay put all night.

Style 1:
"Knot" Your Average Bun

For this style day-old hair is great. This simple do can be done on any length hair. It's cute for daytime and can be dressed up with a headband or jeweled clip for evening.

Step 1: Begin by misting your hair with a light-hold hair spray to add a little texture.

Step 2: Next, run your fingers through your hair, pulling it to the very top of your head.

Step 3: Holding your hair at the top of your head, twist the length all the way to the ends.

Step 4: Wrap the hair around the base in a circular motion. Once a bun shape is formed, secure with a hair elastic. If needed, add some bobby pins to secure any short hair that you may not want sticking up.

Style 2:
The Half Up/Half Down

This is a style I'll often choose when I am wearing a fabulous pair of earrings and I want to show them off. Charles usually leaves the back of my hair "natural" with a little wave scrunched in. But we've also done a braid down one side, or gathered the back into a twist if I want to look good going as well as coming!

What you'll need:

> Brush
>
> Teasing comb
>
> Volumizing mousse
>
> Hair spray
>
> Barrette or hair elastic
>
> Bobby pins

Step 1: To create this look, begin with clean, wet hair. Work a volumizing mousse through your hair, beginning at roots.

Step 2: Part your hair down the middle and blow-dry your hair using a large round brush. Pull your strands upward and concentrate the hair dryer on your roots to create amazing volume. Slightly turn your ends under with the brush.

Step 3: Once your hair is dry, it's time to section it. You want to begin in the back, so using a rattail comb, section out all of the hair from just behind your ears and forward, leaving the sections at each temple down. Next lightly tease the crown of your head (usually the top three or four paper-thin sections.

Step 6: Pin each small section across with bobby pins, making sure to tuck the pin under the hair so it doesn't show. Continue doing this from left to right, crisscrossing each side until just a few strands are left in the front.

Step 7: Finish with a flexible-hold hairspray and a mist of shine spray.

Step 4: Crisscrossing your bobby pins, pin the teased section at the top of your head.

Step 5: Pull the sections still loose toward the teased/pinned hair. The key to this style is to keep the hair very smooth. If your hair tends to frizz, make sure your fingers are slightly coated with sticky pomade (like Pureology's Texture Twist).

Style 3:
The Sophisticated Pony

Yes, I wore ponytails when I was a little girl (didn't we all?), especially for sports and dance. But this looks far more grown-up than my childhood dos. I love the drama of a high pony with supersleek hair—it shows off my cheekbones and makes me feel edgy in an '80s Madonna "Express Yourself" kind of way . . .

What you need:
    Comb/brush
    Curling iron
    Elastic band
    Hair pins
    Hair spray

Step 1: Scoop hair back, smoothing with comb or paddle brush, into a high pony at top of head. Leave a small one-inch section under the pony loose.

Step 2: Take the loose section and wrap it around the base (if you have long hair like mine, you'll need to wrap several times), covering the elastic. You can also braid the section before you wrap it. Secure with bobby pins.

Step 3: You can smooth out the ends with a flat iron or give them a flip with a curling iron. Lightly mist with hair spray to seal the style.

176 *Whitney Port*

skin tone—and it has built-in SPF. I spend hours in Sephora, trying on tons of makeup. Trial and error is the only way to know what looks good on you. My makeup artist, Amy Nadine, also has some great tips and tricks on her Web site (amynadinebeauty.com).

Though it's fun to pick a few new shades each season, you'll probably want to have two complete "go-to" palettes, one for day, one for night.

This is me with just moisturizer and some tinted face cream.

My Five-Minute Face

I'm a big fan of a simple look, and since we don't have a makeup artist on *The City*, I've learned to do my own . . . fast! I know this seems like a lot of steps, but I can do it in just five minutes flat.

Step 1: I start by mixing Fresh High Noon tinted moisturizer with the Fresh Soy Face Cream to get a nice base with a sun-kissed glow.

Step 2: Next I brush on Bare Minerals powder with SPF 15 to even out my skin.

I didn't just get the old Whitney back—this was a new and improved version who cared about her health and fitness. An added incentive: I started shooting *The Hills* in 2005. The camera truly does put

It's your responsibility to keep yourself healthy and happy.

on ten pounds, so I knew that if I wanted to look good—and keep up with the hectic schedule of the show and my *Teen Vogue* internship—I had to be health conscious. As shallow as that may sound, it *did* matter to me.

Luckily, I wised up about my weight before it was too late. And once I was back in shape, I was able to come up with a less drastic diet and a sensible fitness routine (see page 194) to maintain where I'm at. People ask me all the time how I stay slim. The truth is, I don't follow any diet, and I really don't have one type of exercise that whips me into shape. I simply do what works for me, my body, my schedule. And I am a lot more forgiving of myself if I cheat (chocolate-colored Craisins and french fries are my weaknesses), because I know I'm in control now. If I eat something not so healthy for lunch, I can make up for it later on. I'm mindful of what I put in my mouth, which is a far cry from freshman year when my four basic food groups were fat, sugar, salt, and grease!

When you're an adult out on your own, there's no one to remind you to eat your veggies or stop you from snacking before meals. You call the shots. It's your responsibility to keep yourself healthy and happy. If you don't go to the gym or take a yoga class this week, you don't have anyone to answer to except yourself. That's incredibly empowering, because you know that if there's something you don't like about your body, you can change it, just like I did.

MY STAY FIT PHILOSOPHY

People come in all shapes and sizes. Someone can be perfectly fit and comfortable with being a size 12. My comfort zone is somewhere around a size 2/4. I'm tall, so pounds don't show up as easily on me as someone who is shorter. But I believe in eating to increase energy and boosting my immune system—not for calories' sake alone. If you program yourself to think "I am on a diet," you're setting yourself up for defeat. Dieting is restrictive; there's a long list of what you can't eat. It's like wearing a straitjacket!

Instead, I think of it as building a long list of what you *can* and *should* eat. Stuff that will make your skin glow, your body stronger, and ward off wrinkles down the road. I also love that I can get creative (and you know creativity is one of my fave things!) in my meals. I mix it up: some days, I'm all about proteins and veggies, and the next day I want more comfort food. I listen to my body; it knows—probably more than I

do—what it needs. Then I react with some smart choices. If sweetness is what I want, than I don't grab the Häagen-Dazs anymore. Instead, I reach for a sweet potato or a cinnamon raisin English muffin. Or, if I just gotta have chocolate, a sixty-calorie pudding cup or a handful of chocolate-covered Craisins. Satisfaction!

You only live once, and there are just too many things to pass up for the sake of vanity.

I also don't deprive myself. You only live once, and there are just too many things to pass up for the sake of vanity. Usually Sundays are when I indulge a little more. Bread is still my main weakness; I dream of soft Noah's bagels and challah with unsalted butter, and the weekend is when I give in to that craving. One day of bad eating a week isn't going to throw me off. I aim to eat no more than about fifteen hundred calories a day, which is exactly what I need to maintain where I am now. It's a long-term plan that I can live with. The only things I don't eat are red meat, poultry, and pasta—and that's more personal taste than calorie counting. I recently watched the documentary *Food, Inc.* and I literally cannot stomach the thought of eating meat or chicken anymore. I eat with my heart and soul, and to know the processing of the animals is just too much for me to handle. And here's a fun fact: I have *never* eaten pasta in my whole life. Not even when I was a kid—and I know that mac and cheese is the staple of every child's diet. I am very weird about textures in my food, and the sliminess and gooeyness of pasta are just too gross for me! My friends find it a bit freaky; a life sans spaghetti seems strange to them. But I'm happier—and trimmer—because of it!

That's me . . . but what about you? Diet and exercise are personal. You and only you know what feels right for your body. It's never too late or too soon to start being healthier. And there's no one standing in your way at this stage in your life except (you guessed it!) *you*. So many of my friends complain, "I want to lose weight but . . ."

"I want to be in better shape but . . ." There are no buts about it. If you want to be healthy and happy in the future, you have to start thinking about your eating and exercise habits *today*. It's not as simple as just saying, "I won't eat another bagel for the rest of my life." It's strategizing—just as you do in your career, your personal space, or your relationships—where you want to be and who you want to be.

I always try my hardest to make smart choices with food, although if I'm craving something naughty, I'll have a small portion just to settle the craving.

BUILDING YOUR OWN PERSONAL FITNESS PLAN

Think of this as your road map to reaching your goals. Maybe you want to lose twenty pounds . . . or fit into your skinny jeans . . . or have more energy and brighter skin . . . or be more confident. This is your own agenda, no one else's. It's what you want for yourself today and for your future. And now is the time to take responsibility for yourself and your health—you have the power to create whatever kind of life and lifestyle you want, so why not make it a healthy one!

> ## You have the power to create whatever kind of life and lifestyle you want, so why not make it a healthy one!

- Start with a reasonable goal. Losing ten pounds by next Friday is not reasonable! Feeling better and healthier; being stronger and having more energy—these are sensible goals to go for. Write your goal down and pin it up somewhere you can see it every day, like on your fridge or your bathroom mirror. If you need help in setting your goals and strategizing, you can do like I did and seek out a professional trainer or nutritionist. If you can't afford private sessions, ask if the pro will let you and a few friends share the time—or you can also take a group class. Equinox gyms have some awesome group classes at all times.

- Now make a list of the steps you can take *right now* that will help you to achieve this goal. Maybe it's walking to work instead of taking your car. Maybe it's eating five servings of fruits and veggies today and drinking eight glasses of water. Keep it simple. Rome wasn't built in a day, dearie. Think about exercise: What can you do? How often can you do it? Can you get to the gym? How about climbing the stairs in your office instead of taking the elevator? Every little bit adds up.

- As you achieve each step in your plan, check it off and add more to your to-do list. Every "check" is a victory—make sure you celebrate your success and dedication (and I don't mean with a cupcake!). Applaud your efforts by treating yourself to something that's good for you—like a mani/pedi, new hairdo, a sexy new dress. Track your progress—I think writing it down is very helpful, because you can see how far you've come.

- If you have a moment of weakness (don't we all?), don't just give up. Pick yourself up and get back on track tomorrow. I had a few cocktails last night and some bar food, which I know aren't great for me. So today I am refocusing on my fitness plan: I'm having a big salad with ginger dressing for lunch and some fresh fruit for a snack. I feel even stronger when I reaffirm my goals after a momentary lapse. Why? Because I haven't let myself stray too far. I'm in control!

ASK WHITNEY:
WHAT DO YOU EAT . . .

. . . for energy?

I am nuts over nuts—they are my "get up and go" food. They're packed with heart-healthy unsaturated fat, protein, and fiber. I also eat edamame (soy protein), cut-up chunks of Parmesan cheese, or a Fiber One bar. That "fading away feeling" usually hits me around three or four o'clock. Sometimes if I am running around and don't have time, I'll just toss an apple or banana in my bag and munch on it. I get a jolt of vitamin C and fiber (the hunger pangs instantly disappear!). Another plus: eating apples freshens your breath! I am also someone who has to have caffeine. I have coffee in the morning and maybe a Diet Pepsi during the day if I need an extra kick. I know this isn't the best option, but it's one vice I can't kick!

. . . to lose a few pounds fast?

I try not to go on any "crash diet" before a big event or appearance. It's so bad for your body—a real shock to the system—and I don't recommend it. My mentality now is that my diet is a lifestyle choice. That said, there are times when I feel a little "puffy" and want to wear something short, tight, or revealing. To "debloat" I eat lots of greens and fruit, and drink more water. All help rid your body of excess fluid—so you look and feel slimmer.

. . . when you're stressed out?

When you're stressed to excess, you have to put something good in your body. Junk is not going to make you feel less crazed—trust me on this! In fact, the sugar will probably make you feel more hyped up, not calmer. When I'm tense, I reach for a whole-wheat sandwich with banana and peanut butter. It's comforting, satisfying, and filling. I also like to chew things—I think the "crunch" helps me get out some aggression! I am a popcorn person. At home my mom has a big movie theater popcorn maker—she makes it homemade. But I'll just throw a light popcorn pack in the microwave. I even think the yummy smell is aromatherapy for your nerves!

. . . when you're feeling under the weather?

Just recently I felt something "flu-y" coming on. I made a beeline for foods that are high in vitamin C—things like oranges, apples, tomatoes, and broccoli. When I am actually sniffling or sick to my stomach, I love a bowl of vegetable soup and some saltines. I also have a secret-weapon smoothie: there's a vegan place called One Lucky Duck that whips up bananas, almond milk, and cinnamon. It's also great when you're hungover.

Cinnamon Vanilla Banana Shake

Serves 2–4

1 banana
2 cups fat-free milk (I like to use almond milk or cashew milk)
3 tablespoons honey or agave nectar
vanilla extract to taste
ground cinnamon to taste
4 ice cubes

Blend to your desired consistency, and make sure you crush the ice!

MY DAILY MEAL PLAN

I try to eat organic food as much as possible. It makes me feel better physically, and I really like the idea of trying to consume foods that contain as few chemicals and toxins, and as little nonsense, as possible. Roxy and I recently had a fajita night for the Super Bowl. She wanted to get salsa and guacamole in a jar and cook up the veggies with those Mexican seasoning packs. I just couldn't do it. I grew up with everything having to be fresh. I'd rather take the time to chop tomatoes and onions. I'm not a prefabricated girl. My fave new kitchen toy is the Ninja Chopper. You just put in your ingredients and hit a button, and it chops and blends.

Breakfast

One cup 0 percent fat Greek yogurt with chopped unsalted/roasted almonds and chopped Granny Smith apples

The lean dairy protein in yogurt is a great way to kick-start your metabolism in the morning and provides you with a healthy dose of calcium and probiotics for a healthy digestive system. The almonds provide protein, fiber, and healthy mono-unsaturated fats while the apple is a low-glycemic food, packed with fiber so it helps fill you up until lunchtime.

Or

An egg white omelet with onions/mushrooms/spinach, side of whole-wheat toast. The protein of the egg and veggies will give you energy.

Or

Cinnamon raisin English muffin toasted with peanut butter and chopped bananas.

Lunch

Spinach salad with garbanzo beans, avocado, tomatoes, and a little shaved Parmesan with Girard's lite champagne dressing

Or

Classic PBJ on whole-grain toast. The toast is a source of filling fiber and heart-healthy whole grains; peanut butter is packed with protein.

Or

Whole-wheat English muffin toasted and topped with avocado and melted Parmesan cheese, with a side of tomato soup.

To maintain bikini-ready bods, Roxy and I eat healthy and organic food.

Afternoon Snack Options

- Natural, lightly salted Orville Redenbacher's popcorn
- Jell-O sixty-calorie vanilla/chocolate pudding packs
- Apple and peanut butter
- Banana and a handful of almonds (approximately 24)
- Cup of pea soup

Dinner

These are some favorites for a low-key night in. When I go out, I try to eat a lot of veggies and watch out for sauces that can pack way more calories than they're worth.

- Veggie burger with a side of roasted broccoli and edamame
- Lentil soup with a healthy grains salad and nondairy dressing
- Steamed artichoke, roasted sweet potatoes, and any kind of white fish/tuna tartare

MY EXERCISE PLAN

I admit it . . . I have body envy. I wish I could look like Gisele Bündchen (don't we all?). But I work hard and use those perfect bodies as inspiration. Working out is good for both body and soul. It makes you feel stronger, more energetic. It makes your body function more efficiently—your lungs and heart become more powerful. Look, I don't love everything about my body. I've got some extra loving on my love handles that I could do without, and I'd love to have slimmer arms. But I try to focus on the positives: I like my legs, and I am starting to embrace my 32D boobs. My trainer, Danny Connolly, puts me through the paces and helps me stay lean and mean. I'm by no means an exercise junkie, but I do try to hit the gym three times a week or, at the very least, run through some of these exercises at home for twenty minutes each day. In a pinch, I'll just squeeze in some push-ups and sit-ups.

Note: Of course, you shouldn't do these exercises if you have any injuries or disabilities. You should always consult your doctor before beginning an exercise program.

My trainer, Danny Connolly.

Weighted Squats

Repeat 10–25 reps total.

1. Establish a slightly wider than hip-width stance with the toes turned slightly outside of the heels.
2. Grasp a kettle ball or dumbbell with a light to moderate weight (10–15 lbs) and allow the weight to hang below the chin with the arms in a straight or locked elbow position.
3. Tilt the hips in a backward direc-

tion and lower the hips and glutes backward and down into a squat. Don't allow the knees to drift over the path of the toes.

4. Keep the upper torso as erect and tall as possible, and press heels into the ground as you raise yourself back up. To make the exercise more challenging, pause longer at the lowest position.

Bench Push-ups

Push-ups are very challenging on the arms and particularly on the core. Start with sets of 5–10, and work up to 3 sets of 15 with minimal rest (1–2 minutes) between sets.

1. Place hands on bench and place the feet fairly close together to target the core. Start in the upper position of the push-up. (For beginners, perform this on a high bench.)

2. Slowly lower the upper torso down toward the bench, while allowing the elbows to drift in a straight line outward. (The wider the elbows, the more overall benefit of the exercise. When the elbows drift inward/toward the sides of the body, the triceps work harder).

3. Draw the tummy in as you lower yourself down to reap maximum benefit on the abs!

4. Return to the upper position and exhale on the way up.

Triceps Dip on a Bench

This is another effective move to combat flabby arms and can be performed anywhere—wherever a chair, ledge, or a bench is available. To see maximum results, Danny recommends doing at least 3 sets of 10–15 reps, 3 days a week.

1. Grasp a bench with an overhand grip; the arms should be about shoulder-width apart.
2. The farther away the feet are, the more challenging the move. For beginners, place the feet underneath the knees, which should be bent. For the more advanced, the legs can be straight out in front of you to enhance the work on the arms and shoulders.

3. Slowly lower the upper torso down along a straight path. The spine should stay relatively close to the bench the entire way down.
4. Pause at the lowest position and reverse the direction by utilizing the upper arm/triceps to propel the body up again.
5. Lock the elbows and squeeze the triceps at the top and then repeat 10–15 reps. For an extra challenge, alternate lifting each leg.

Alternating Tow with Leg Up

This move is awesome for arms! It targets the lats, rear delts, biceps, as well as your core (abs of steel!).

1. Balance yourself by placing one hand on a bench or other support.
2. Grasp a dumbbell or kettle ball with one arm and raise the alternate leg up to a parallel position. (The higher the leg, the more the butt and hips will be targeted.)
3. Allow the weight to hang naturally below the shoulder, as you attempt to draw in the abs for additional support. (Inhale prior to lifting the weight and *exhale* as you begin raising the weight.)

4. Raise the weight by pulling through the *elbow*, not the hand. The elbow directly "ties in" to the shoulders and lats and creates more leverage. The elbow should lift the weight by pulling up and *back* toward the hip. (The closer the elbow is to the hip and rib cage, the more beneficial.)

5. Pause at the uppermost position, and lower slowly back down. At-
   p the leg up as high
   arallel to the ground
   effectiveness.
   times per side (2 or 3

Waistline Chops with Tension Band

I like doing this move with Danny tossing me a weighted ball. It targets all the muscles along the waistline as well as the shoulders and upper arms.

1. Stand with a hip-width foot position and attach a tension band at about shoulder level to a support.

2. Holding the tension band, straighten the arms and lock the elbows. (The straighter the arm, the more effective the move).

3. Rotate the upper torso *only*, attempting to keep the hips and butt in a stationary or "static" position, as the arms, shoulders, and so on pivot to approximately a three o'clock or nine o'clock position, depending on the direction traveled. Danny tells me to visualize keeping the belly button in a stationary position as everything *above* it rotates.

4. Pause for a moment before returning to the original position. Repeat 15–25 times per side, alternating sides between sets. For more tension, and to make the move more challenging, step farther away from the support.

Single-Arm Warrior Rows

These are performed using the tension bands with one arm or two. This is a great exercise to do when traveling or to target multiple body parts. Beginners can perform the exercise in a seated position as well.

1. Place a tension band around a support and step back into a Warrior 1 Position stance (legs in a lunge position with the back foot flat on the ground at a forty-five-degree angle). The more depth one can get with the back/front legs, the more effective the move. The farther back the foot position, the better.

2. Pull with the elbows in a downward and backward arc until the elbows are as far back as they can comfortably go. Pause there.

3. Slowly release the tension and make sure to keep the elbows as close to the sides as possible.

4. Repeat 12–20 reps with each leg in the back position.

Bent-Over Kickbacks

This exercise really works triceps, hips, and thighs.

1. Grasp a pair of 3- to 5-pound dumbbells or place a tension band around a support and assume a "ski-jumper" position by bending forward at the waist. Begin with a bent arm position with the upper arm parallel to the floor. Elbows should be even with the shoulders throughout the entire range of motion.

2. Extend the arms in a straight and backward path and pause there.

3. Slowly return to the starting position while not allowing the elbows to drift down.

4. For maximum effectiveness, perform some extensions with the upper arms away from the sides. This places more pressure on the shoulders. Do 2 or 3 sets of 10–30 reps with minimal rest between sets.

Biceps Curls in the Warrior Position

1. Place a tension band around a support and step back into a Warrior 1 Position.
2. Raise the elbows up to increase the tension on the shoulders and the biceps.
3. Keep the elbows and upper arms in a parallel position to the floor as you curl the tension band by bringing the wrists to the forehead. Squeeze the biceps at this position before returning to the starting position. Keep the elbows up and the upper arm parallel throughout the entire set. (To increase the intensity, step farther away from the support and/or go deeper in the knees to burn the thighs more!)
4. Perform 10–15 reps before switching legs. Do 3 sets of 20–30 reps total.

Inner Thigh, Glute, and Hip Elevations

This move works wonders to tone the hips, glutes, and inner thighs, all at the same time! It can be performed with or without a ball between the knees.

1. Lay flat on your back with the knees bent and the feet placed slightly in front of the knees.
2. Place a soft ball between the knees and squeeze it gently. Before you begin raising or thrusting the hips up toward the sky/ceiling, squeeze the knees together forcefully as you attempt to squeeze the ball, too.

3. Now raise the hips and glutes up off the floor and attempt to contract those muscles as you continue to apply pressure to the knees and ball.
4. Release some pressure on the ball as you lower the hips and butt back down to the ground. Repeat 12–15 times.

Don't forget to stretch!

CHAPTER EIGHT

DESIGNING WOMAN

Most girls dream of being something fun and fabulous when they grow up: a rock star, a supermodel, a five-star chef. For me, it was always a fashion designer. My entire life, I've had a deep love and admiration for fashion, and a desire to do something creative and original. But it wasn't until I hit my twenties and I was working at DVF, actually observing the designing process from start to finish, that I began to think, Well, what am I waiting for?

Your twenties are the ideal time to try your dream on for size. At this point, you have college and some practical work experience already under your belt (in my case, I had six years of working behind the scenes in fashion). You usually don't have a ton of responsibilities yet like a family and a mortgage weighing on your shoulders, and if it doesn't pan out, you have plenty of time to try a different path and still have a successful career. Try not to let your personal fears or lack of funds hold you back. You can always start small and build your biz. I also think it's really important to have a job while you're starting your own business. It's a little safety net; just be prepared to put in long hours and kiss some of your social life good-bye while you burn the midnight

Your twenties are the ideal time to try your dream on for size.

oil. I really never imagined how much work starting my line would be—it's all-consuming! That said . . . it's totally worth it. There is nothing more fulfilling and thrilling than making your dream a reality.

STEP 1:
BELIEVE IN YOURSELF

Like the Little Engine That Could, you have to look in the mirror and say, "I think I can, I think I can." Even if you have lots of people pulling for you like I do, in the end, you are the one taking the risk and putting yourself out there. You are the one who will stand or fall based on your own merit. I'll be honest—this really terrified me. What if I was deluding myself all these years? What if I didn't have what it takes to be a successful designer? What if I was too young and inexperienced to do something so big on my own. Sure, I could wait, but I didn't really know what I was waiting for. A guarantee? Life doesn't have many of those, and the fashion world certainly doesn't.

I was a grown-up now and I had to be practical. So I weighed the pros and cons.

Pros: I could become a world-famous designer with my own line of affordable, fabulous clothing for young women!

Cons: My collection could be a big fat failure and I could go broke and die of embarrassment trying (one of the joys of living your life on a reality TV show!).

I went to one of the smartest people I know, Kelly Cutrone, and presented my dilemma. Kelly cut right to the chase (as I knew she would): "Whitney, if you want to do it, *just do it*!" Was it really that simple? Was having the desire enough? I reminded Kelly I had never gone to design school; I couldn't even sew! But she convinced me that what I needed to know wasn't necessarily found in books—it would come from practical, hands-on experience. She offered me the chance to work for her part-time while I designed my first collection. And when I was ready, she said she'd help me get it in front of the right buyers. But she also warned me that I might fail . . . big time. There are tons of really talented designers out there who never make it in the fashion industry. Fashion is very fickle; you can be "in" today and on the return rack tomorrow. "It's a lot of work, and it may not happen for you," Kelly warned. "But then again, you won't know unless you try, right?"

STEP 2: THE BIG IDEA

What are you going to make/do? Define your product(s) for both yourself and potential future investors. What is it about your product that is different? Fresh? New? Why will it sell? To whom will it appeal? Kelly asked me these things when we first spoke, and it really forced me to think about why my line would be different from all the other labels out there (and there are literally *thousands*!). It's a good idea to picture the person who will be wearing/using your product. In the beginning I was designing for me and my friends. I felt like there was something missing in the fashion industry, so I was mixing the L.A. vibe (laid-back) with the NYC vibe (sophisticated) and creating a fun party-girl line. Later on, I realized I couldn't just think about what *I* would want; I had to really think about designing for different people from many different places who are many different sizes. Today, my consumer is a twenty-five-year-old woman who has a modest income but is and wants to look fashion-forward.

STEP 3: BE TRUE TO YOU

Don't copy what everyone else is doing just because you think it will sell. Show some originality. I knew my line was not going to look like everything else out there; I wanted it to reflect my own personal style, which is flirty, feminine, and a bit unconventional. I wanted it to feel fresh and new, rather than playing it safe. But in

Sketching and painting were always hobbies of mine growing up—a real fashion designer in the making!

fashion, that can be a huge risk. Buyers—especially in this economy—want to fill the stores with "sure things." They don't want to take a chance on something they've never seen before. I knew this, but I also knew that I couldn't design anything that wasn't 100 percent Whitney. It's why I named my line Whitney Eve (Eve is my middle name).

STEP 4: YOU GOTTA HAVE A PLAN

It's a lot of fun to be spontaneous and "wing it" but not when it comes to your business. You have to have a firm plan of action. What are you going to do? When are you going to do it? What will it cost? How much time will it take? In fashion, designers always work several months in advance. So when you see a line in stores, that line has been made months and months in advance. For example, my Fall 2010 line will be in stores in August, but I had to have all my samples done by the first week of February! So I am always planning ahead, jotting down ideas for what I want to do down the road. I look at what's in style now . . . and I try to give it a fresh new twist. It's a lot of guesswork; a lot of hit and miss. But the more you do it, the more you learn to trust your instincts.

In drawing up a business plan, you should also do your homework: research the competition; production and delivery costs; potential vendors; and your fixed costs—like office space or a new computer or a phone line if you need one. It's a good idea to protect your idea with a patent or copyright (in my case, we had to make sure no one was using the name Whitney Eve). If you don't have a friend, parent, or mentor you can ask for advice, you can also contact the U.S. Small Business Administration or SCORE (score.org) for free business counseling.

STEP 5: BE READY TO DEAL WITH MONEY, HONEY

Budgeting is not something I do best. You'll need to budget for all your initial start-up costs and also the continuing costs of raw material and labor to keep the company going.

My dad is the voice of reason when it comes to planning the financial side of my business. Because he's in the fashion trade, he knows how pricey it can be to manufacture clothing. So as I am cheerfully picking out these beautiful, expensive fabrics and trims for my samples, he'll remind me this will drive up the price of each piece in stores—which is something I want to avoid.

Before you get started, you're going to have to juggle some figures and see where you stand. Consider whether you will need financial backing. I had saved up money from all my jobs, so I was prepared to invest my own money in producing my first samples. If you don't have the cash, be cautious about piling up debt. Start small. As your biz builds, you can always

pursue some investors. My best tip: don't quit your day job. Make sure you have an income while you're working on your new business. That way, you can support yourself if you have to deplete a lot of your nest egg.

My dad and brother at a sales convention in Las Vegas called Project.

My dad has been in the fashion industry forever, so I always look to him for advice.

STEP 6: SPREAD THE WORD

You don't need to take out a billboard in Times Square. Start by giving some of your product to a few friends and asking them to wear it out. I was so happy when Roxy wore one of my silver sequin jackets from the new Fall collection to my karaoke birthday party the other night. The key is to pound the pavement and get your stuff out there. Have a trunk show; create a Web site; take your stuff into stores. These are all things you can do for little or no money. Call some editors at magazines and ask if you can send in samples—or even dash off a few pieces to a fave celebrity's publicist.

I get items from new designers all the time. And guess what? If I love it, I'm going to wear it. Instant advertising! I was able to get my line into a showroom, which is great—because they market it for you and take it to buyers and conventions around the country. True, I have to give up a percentage of my sales to the showroom for doing this, but if you're busy, it's a great solution for taking your biz broader.

Two designs from my Fall 2010 collection.

STEP 7: DON'T GIVE UP

If at first you don't succeed, don't dump your dream. I went through a ton of disappointments before my line landed on the runway and in stores. The greatest blow was Bergdorf's—which everyone got to see on *The City*. The buyers were very nice when I showed them my first samples, but they clearly thought I had a lot of learning left to do and weren't ready to carry my line in their NYC store. Oh, well. In retrospect, they were right. I think each one of my collections gets better and better, and I know so much more now than I did when I was first starting out. But at that moment, it did feel like the end of the world and I doubted I would ever make it as a designer. Thank God for Kelly, who once again put it all in perspective for me. Just because one door closes, it doesn't mean there aren't hundreds of others to knock on. I kept plugging away, and by some miracle (and many sleepless nights) I was able to show an entire collection of 30-plus looks at Bryant Park.

To be an entrepreneur, you have to develop a tough skin. You can't take the criticism and rejection to heart; it's not personal, it's business. Not everyone is going to like what you do or choose to buy your product, and that's okay. You have to own the risk—then you can own the success as well.

A SEASON IN THE LIFE . . .
WHITNEY AS DESIGNER!

Sketching My Line

An average fashion show requires at least thirty looks—but that means a lot more pieces, since you're putting together tops and bottoms. My first step is to sketch the individual pieces so I can begin to see what will mix and match well together.

When you're a designer, you have to look into the future. I wish I had a crystal ball, but I don't. I have to just follow my gut.

Sketches and photos from my Fall 2010 line.

2/10 ①

#1
SE INC.

R #2
A

SLEEVE COLOR

SLEEVE + E
COLOR #
LAGUNA

MIDDLE SE
STRETCH HOU
$6 yd

#1
T

BODY COL
LAGUNA

IPING/SLEEV
STRETCH HO
$8 yd

blk

COLOR WAY #
STRETCH HOUSE
$16 yd

TRIMMING
COLOR WAY.
B+Q
12 yd.

WAY #1
O FABRICS INC
$?

AY #2
GO FABRICS IN
$?

Y#3

WAY #4
HOUSE INC
yd

blk

Finding Fabrics

I comb the Fashion District going through rolls of fabrics and trimmings. I even pick the buttons and sequins myself! It's fun, but a tremendous amount of searching—a little like looking for a needle in a haystack sometimes.

Creating Samples

I meet with sample makers and pattern-makers to give them the technical sketches in order to start cutting and sewing. I pick out a bunch of fabrics, and we decide which ones will work for which piece. This is a really important decision—you can't make something loose and flowy out of a tough wool!

The Look Book

After a long process (at least six months to a year) of correcting samples and fitting them on models, it's time to show the market what I've designed! I put together my "Look Book" so buyers and fashion editors can get a feel for what I am offering for the season. I hire a model, a photographer, and stylists to create a minicatalog of digital images. Then we can e-mail them anywhere and everywhere!

Working with my patternmaker, Margarett.

Behind the scenes at my Look
Book photo shoot.

fall
2010

whitney eve
COLLECTION

Showing on the Runway

No one will know how great your collection is unless you show it. So twice a year, we try to organize a presentation or runway show to unveil my latest designs. I recently took part in the Gen Art Fresh Faces in Fashion show in Miami where I showed my Fall 2010 collection—along with five other new designers—to a huge

Backstage and onstage at the Gen Art show.

crowd. Although the idea of putting on a runway show sounds glam, a lot of hard work and detail go into it. At a show, the designer does much more than create the clothing; she or he has to see the entire show through production. I have to cast the models; decide on hair, makeup, lighting, and music; style all the looks with accessories; arrange for the line to be transported; send out invites; and make the all-important call—who gets to sit in the front two rows of the show. *Phew!* To get everything perfect, we do a run-through. And even then, when the real show rolls around, it's chaos backstage! My heart is always racing, but I try to focus on things going smoothly—not my nerves. Besides, I really don't have time to worry—the show flies by in about fifteen to twenty minutes.

Hitting the Stores

Immediately after the show, my samples get sent to the showroom that carries my line for buyers to look at or the sales team takes them on the road for me, bringing them to boutiques, department stores, and trade conventions (Project is the big one in Vegas; Coterie in New York City). Hopefully, they get lots of orders and that helps us determine how much to produce. When I actually see my looks on racks or shelves in stores . . . that's the ultimate reward!